Sagittarius

The Ultimate Guide to an Amazing Zodiac Sign in Astrology

Contents

Introduction

The mysteries of the zodiac are all around us, but deep within the core of our personalities, our sun signs connect us with the universe. If you are a Sagittarius or know one, you can dive deep into the passionate fire sign with this guide. Our complete guide explores what it means to be a Sagittarius, how the planetary movements affect you, and what challenges you'll meet throughout life. You'll have the opportunity to understand more about Ophiuchus, the evasive sign residing within your house and explore the context of being born to the Ninth House of the zodiac and being ruled under Jupiter.

As a Sagittarius, you might have noticed key strengths and weaknesses. Learn more about what those mean for you in daily life, and how you can address them head-on. Sagittarians love to explore, wander, learn, and speak their mind. You can live your best life and feed into these aspects of your core personality. Sagittarians have the chance to rule the world and lead a strong group of diverse friends forward through life as a guide and mentor. As a natural leader with a deep passion for freedom, you'll find that people come to Sagittarians for a variety of reasons. With enhanced knowledge about yourself or the Sagittarius native in your life, you will adapt your approach to various life obstacles and use your strengths to keep you moving toward the future with the classic Sagittarian positive mindset.

Chapter 1: Sagittarius in the Zodiac

Over 4,000 years ago, a combination of overarching beliefs came together. Romans, Egyptians, and ancient Babylonians had independently charred the heavens into the same findings. When Rome and ancient Egypt came together, they combined their findings to chart the stars with a mathematical and scientific foundation. This was the birth of astronomy. These civilizations brought together their mythologies and understanding of the heavens to deliver the zodiac we know today. Through many thousand years of research and tracking planetary movements, and personality traits and changes, astrology eventually split from astronomy.

All three civilizations identified the 12 houses and the 12 constellations that would rule the zodiac in the thousands of years to come. This is the same zodiac we know and use today. Astrology plays a large part in our lives, regardless of how much people do or don't believe it. We're all in the universe together, and those who understand and acknowledge the widespread network of connection can understand their strengths, overcome weaknesses, and plan their daily lives for the best possible outcomes.

Astrology has waxed and waned through the centuries, but it has always been present in our societies. Even when belief was at an all-time low, the zodiac and the time of year we're born impact our personalities and our daily lives.

In this book, you'll can explore the Sagittarius zodiac sign and what it means to live as a Sagittarian. This book isn't exclusively for those born to the sign. It can help anyone better understand a Sagittarian friend, sibling, child, parent, romantic partner, or even coworker.

Here you will have access to not only an in-depth look at Sagittarius but the impact of the movements of the planets, and moon signs, rising signs, as well as the two forms of Sagittarian cusps.

Mythological Origins of Sagittarius

Sagittarius's mythical origins vary from Babylonian belief, Roman belief, Greek belief, and Sumerian mythology. It is easy to see a connection between each story and how it may have adapted over the years. There are also clear similarities that play into the beliefs behind the Sagittarius personality, although each civilization had a different angle when the personality was reviewed.

Among Babylonian mythology, Sagittarius was acknowledged as the *centauresque* God Nergal. Sagittarius among the Babylonians had a horse-like body, human-like torso, wings, the scorpion of a Stinger poised above the horse's tail, and two heads, one human and one panther. Nergal often is shown representing war and scorched earth.

Romans had a different approach to Sagittarius. They used the root of the word the Sagitta, which means arrow. Initially enroll, many observers identified a teapot among the constellation, but eventually, The Archer's bow and arrow won out, and the constellation was declared Sagittarius.

Eratosthenes, one of history's best-known astronomers, pushed that the constellation was a satyr rather than a Centaur. This was another term for Sagittarius because it was through storytelling that the center motif we know now came to form. The legend of Sagittarius among Roman mythology is that Crotus was the son of Pan, and he lived atop Mount Helicon and invented archery. Eventually, Sagittarius was placed among the stars when the muses requested it of Zeus.

The connection between the muses and Sagittarius appears again in Greek mythology. Sagittarius is still shown as a centaur or as a half-human and half-horse creature. But in Greek mythology, the centaur was a nurse to the muses, and played careful watchman to guard them. Sagittarius is identified as aiming his arrow towards the heart of Scorpio. This story is like the beliefs among Sumerian mythology.

Basics of Being a Sagittarius

What makes a Sagittarius? Sagittarians are born between November 22nd and December 21st. They are the 9th sign within the zodiac circle, and they're symbolized through the Archer, who is aiming his bow at the higher realms of life.

To offer a clear overview, here are the most present and forceful elements within Sagittarius:

- Fire sign

- Mutable modality

- Assertive duality

- Ninth house of the zodiac

- Ruled under Jupiter

- The power colors are blue and purple

- Represents potential health risks within the liver, hips, and thighs

- Represented as the carnation

- Stones include turquoise, blue zircon, topaz, and citrine

Overall, Sagittarians are the most curious and energetic personalities among the zodiac's personas. They are also known for their love of travel, open-mindedness, and strong philosophical opinions. They are the people who ask the big questions. They want to know the meaning of life and explore their purpose.

Of course, that is the big picture image of a Sagittarius. On a personal level, they are often extroverted, enthusiastic, easy to excite, optimistic, and they enjoy change. Their mutable modality tied with their fire element make them extremely passionate about what lies ahead for them.

The mutable modality is what makes them so excited about the change. At the same time, the fire element gives them that drive to seek it out rather than the other elements with the same modality. Sagittarius is not a war between any of its present factors, such as its modality, element, planet, or house. These all come together nicely for Sagittarius, so it's likely that they'll feel at peace within themselves most of the time, but they may have a hard couple of years as a teenager while they're still figuring this out.

As a final note for the overview of Sagittarius, they value freedom above all other things. That love of freedom is best shown through famous Sagittarian John Jay. Jay is among the twelve most well-known founding fathers of the United States, the first United States Chief of Justice of the Supreme Court. He helped lead the changes that formed America following the Revolutionary War, and in 1799, he proved he was an advocate of widespread change by freeing all slaves within New York. John Jay is one example, but history has countless figures who stand out as those who put their highest value on freedom, honesty, and change.

Born to Jupiter

One of Sagittarians' most defining aspects is that they're born under Jupiter and how closely that connects with their fire element. The planet Jupiter is the largest of the celestial bodies, excluding the sun.

Many in astrology idealize Jupiter for its benevolent and beneficial nature. This planet brings a lot of hope into Sagittarians.

Jupiter represents growth, expansion, healing, miracles, good fortune, and higher education. For Sagittarians, this planet marks the core of their personality, and it often means they see the world through those classic rose-colored glasses. Jupiter is the reason so many Sagittarians experience such high levels of enthusiasm and optimism.

The Mutable of the Fire Signs

Mutable signs come in the time of year when change is imminent. Of course, fire is the element of passion, and after fall, there is a passion for change to enter the season of quiet, death, and rebirth. Sagittarians aren't afraid of facing hardship or rough times. They will still charge ahead and stay the course, knowing that change is the only thing that will end the hardship in front of them.

This deep desire and the acceptance that change comes in many ways contributes to the Sagittarian optimism. Sagittarians do look forward to the winter and see it as a season of purpose. They aren't looking at winter as the season of hardship but are looking to it as the bridge to reach springtime, birth, and revitalization.

Sagittarius: the Final Fire Sign

Each element presents a trio of zodiac signs, and where the signs fall within that trio indicates how that element impacts that sign. Sagittarius is the last of the fire signs. It's preceded by Aries and Leo. To give context, areas as the first fire sign is like the ignition of a fire or that slow crackle that happens with kindling. Leo often represents fire in a full blaze in its purest form.

Sagittarius is the final fire sign that presents something uplifting, it is the slow burn, and it's through this that Sagittarians can often carry out monumental feats. They train themselves to have long stretches of energy rather than short bursts of energy or moderate energy levels and rest that come with Leo. Of the three fire signs, they are known for their generosity, and outshine both Leo and Aries when it comes to being generous and working with good intentions.

As a fire sign, they are often more compassionate and hold a deeper understanding of the human condition. They are often compelled to give more than they can and struggle between the desire to be more generous and their ability to do so.

The Sagittarius level of generosity is often a surprise to other signs. Sagittarians often give much more than people see, and unlike Aries and Leo, they aren't quick to jump for recognition for their generosity. They may even seem hesitant to make commitments or go through with plans, and that's because they've overwhelmed themselves with obligations wanting to volunteer their time and energy. There's also the widespread idea that Sagittarius is our flighty or non-committal. Their flightiness is their wish for change, and their non-committal attitude often exposes their underlying feelings or opinions about this person. If a Sagittarius can provide their time, energy, or money, then their flightiness and their level of commitment can drastically change.

Sagittarian Men and Women

Fire signs have larger differences between men and women than the other elements. With earth signs, you can guarantee that both sexes are pretty much grounded. Fire signs burn in different ways.

First, Sagittarius men are classically idealistic and opportunistic. They exude this innocence and can come across as annoying or childish. They often work in blind faith and trust just about anyone, which can cause a lot of unfortunate outcomes, especially when dealing with romance and business. Male Sagittarius are less in tune with Jupiter's logic element, but are more aligned with Jupiter's spark of curiosity.

Sagittarius men also receive the upper hand in Jupiter's gift of luck. They may go through long stretches of unluckiness, and that is typically a lesson they need. This lesson allows them to learn that they can't rely on good things to come their way. And they have no tolerance for dishonesty or inconsistent behavior. This is exceptionally noticeable when they are children. They need parents who are consistent in expectations and discipline.

The other side of Sagittarius men is their sense of humor and their ability to make friends. They quick to make friends, whether they want them or not. They have these magnetic personalities which just pull people in, but all Sagittarians are also prone to the foot-in-mouth syndrome. They often say things too bluntly or are too forthcoming with their opinions when they don't have knowledge on the subject. Sagittarius men are often blessed with the gift of humor and can deliver these overly blunt opinions or insight through the mode of comedy. This gift allows them to keep many more friends than Sagittarius women may experience.

On the downside, men under this sign are also prone to thoughtlessness and scattered thinking. They may have big dreams and want to help cultivate long-lasting change, but unless they have someone to guide them through those changes or help them achieve that goal, it may take much longer than it should. These men need a guiding light and constant reminders of why they're working on a particular project.

Sagittarius women, on the other hand, apply logic ruthlessly and are more prone to accept the general structure of an organization than Sagittarius men. These are the women who know what needs to be done to accomplish the big goals and achieve big change. The struggle they face boils down to communication.

As mentioned earlier, Sagittarians often struggle with being too blunt and too straightforward. This challenge is even more difficult for these women. A Sagittarius woman is the one who will ask embarrassing questions in Group settings, speak inappropriately often, and be disarmingly honest, but many make this a strength rather than a challenge. They use their honesty and frankness to catch others off-guard. One particular Sagittarian celebrity has made a reputation of this, Chrissy Teigen is well known for expressing her opinion unapologetically an all matter of the public forum. The trick here for these ladies is to decide whether this is a challenge you must overcome or a strength you will embody in everyday life.

Women under this sign are extraordinarily independent. Not necessarily that they live alone or are abject to family life, but they see themselves as individuals who contribute to various groups rather than a person subjected to labels and roles.

Understanding Sagittarian Cusps

Every person on a cusp has a bit of a different twist when it comes to their zodiac signs and what you might expect from their core personality. Sagittarius cusps struggle because one is a water-fire combination, and the other is an air-fire combination.

The Scorpio to Sagittarius cusp combines water and fire. Although these two normally contradict, their level of intensity is what makes the Scorpio-Sagittarius cusp widely successful. Traditionally, Scorpio was ruled under Mars and known for action, although the modern zodiac shows Scorpio represented through Pluto with a deep psychic connection and ties to death. When you take that and bring it together with Sagittarius, you have someone who is very open and receptive to change while also prone to take the necessary action to achieve their goals.

Those born on the Scorpio to Sagittarius cusp are more likely to see widespread success, but they may have difficulty in keeping friends. They will make friends quickly like all other Sagittarius is, but will probably lose them a little faster because of their matter-of-fact way of telling things and that extra dose of anger they get from their Scorpio side.

When it comes to downsides, the Scorpio-Sagittarius cusp often brings quite a bit of a know-it-all attitude, and these people can quickly become overly self-righteous. They may deliver truth bombs when inappropriate and obsessively dive into the research to make sure that they are right about something long after the conversation or argument has ended.

On the other side of the sign is the Sagittarius-Capricorn cusp, which ranges from December 18th to the 24th. These visionaries have a strong grasp on prophecy and how to propel change and control the direction of change to accomplish that prophecy. Capricorns are known for their intense determination and stubborn or headstrong nature. Inherently, this seems to contradict the Sagittarian's want for change and a go with the flow approach to life. It's possible that a Sagittarius-Capricorn cusp could get the best of both worlds. They could understand limits and lessons which come from Capricorn's planetary rulers of Saturn and support that curiosity and need for change associated with Jupiter and their modality. The trouble is that it is *just as likely* they will receive the worst of both worlds. Then they could be stubborn and overly blunt with their opinions. They may be intensely determined to prove others wrong and drive away many friends.

Those born in the Sagittarius-Capricorn cusp range are often carrying, loyal, and reasonable. They apologize frequently but also answering questions and giving advice.

Being Sagittarius

The elements that play a role in being a Sagittarius make up specific portions of your core personality. As a whole, Sagittarians are friendly, curious, adventurous, and fun people.

As you read your way through this book, you'll see how the different elements of being a Sagittarius play into different aspects of your life, such as childhood, romance, career pathways, and more. But your element, modality, and the sign itself don't independently determine your personality. Sagittarius is your sun sign and the essence of yourself. But other planetary movements and planetary presences within your natal can affect you too. How the universe impacts your path always comes to viewing and experiencing life through the lens of a Sagittarius.

Chapter 2: Who are Sagittarians?

Sagittarians don't hide who they are, and they're unapologetic in almost every aspect of their life. Those born to Sagittarius have a purpose in life, and they know that drive to explore and defy boundaries defines who they are through all stages of life. They don't adhere to standard conventions, and they actively seek information that may contradict a few of society's core beliefs. They are the people who ask questions; they want to know why and why not. Sagittarians are the truth-seekers of the Zodiac.

They need for knowledge, curiosity, and exploration all comes down to their ruling planet Jupiter. Jupiter's flow of energy focuses on the higher mind, expansion, and good fortune. You'll have the opportunity to learn a bit more about Jupiter, but it's key to mention that right initially because of what an important role it plays in their life.

There's also the need to mention the modality of Sagittarius. As a mutable sign, they often go with the flow and have a good-humored or jovial nature about them. These are just a few of the many strengths or benefits that come with being a Sagittarius. In this chapter, you'll have an introduction to those strengths, a handful of the challenges they face, and the overall view or big picture of who Sagittarians are in life.

What Does it Mean to be a Sagittarius?

At first sight, it looks as though being a Sagittarius just means you were born between November 22nd and December 21st, but those familiar with the sign will know that Sagittarians are fiercely independent, good-humored, charming, and occasionally, annoyingly optimistic. Sagittarius born also tend to be sent mental and quick to anger. At their worst times, they may seem inconsiderate or overreact too small events.

Many of the most remarkable traits found with Sagittarius natives are their ability to be blunt, philosophical, and extraordinarily independent. Those born to this sign are more than a little outspoken. They will often lead conversations in the direction they want to put out their ideas and opinions. And Sagittarius people often find themselves in friendly debates. The keyword is friendly. Because of their open-mindedness, Sagittarians are widely accepting of differing opinions and views. Part of the underlying element with this bluntness and this outspokenness is the Sagittarian's drive for truth and learning. They take a "truth hurts" approach to philosophical, political, and social subjects. Those born to Sagittarius don't consider her brothers anyone out there who can't handle the truth. They believe everyone needs to hear it and will do everything possible to spread the word.

What often causes a conflict for Sagittarians is their need for picking apart abstract views and philosophical ideas. They like the concept of aspects of life not having clear answers, but they hate not finding the one answer. This contradiction helps them continue growing and is often why Sagittarians are lifelong learners.

All the elements of Sagittarius we've addressed above stem from two key factors of this sign. Their ruling planet of Jupiter, and their element of fire, but it's their modality that presents the final element of the over-arching Sagittarius personality. When people look at Sagittarius on a surface level, they often see extreme independence or outright restlessness. Sagittarians need personal freedom like we all need air, and it's because of their mutable quality.

The mutable modality is what drives the need for change, and it happened when seasons change. Sagittarius marks the end of fall and the beginning of winter. Those born under Sagittarius are looking to the forthcoming, and when they're tied down, they think that the future will only hold the same thing that they've been experiencing. Sagittarians are not necessarily averse to long-term relationships, and they cultivate long-term friendships well. The trouble is that when things stop changing and being new, the Sagittarian checks out. For those born to Sagittarius, they see it as a "been there, done that" situation.

For example, if a Sagittarius has had a friend for a long time, and they've seen that friend frequently go in and out of the same bad relationship, they might end their friendship. In this example, the Sagittarius will not have much patience for hearing about the same problems again and again. They won't be very accepting of their friends, being incapable of moving forward. Because of this low tolerance for repetition and their drive to live without restraint, it looks as though Sagittarius men and women have trouble cultivating relationships.

These elements of a Sagittarius personality are tied into the Sagittarius element, modality, ruling planet, and Association with planetary movements. Although astrology is not widely accepted as a science, there is more astronomy that plays a role in understanding your sun sign and its impact on your day-to-day life. It is easy to say that Sagittarius natives are usually dependable and open-minded. Those observations are surface level. Throughout this book, and starting in this chapter, you'll have the opportunity to look at the in-depth analysis necessary to understand planetary movements, sun signs, moon signs, and how the universe affects you.

Understand Your Different Signs

To start things out, being a Sagittarius is your core personality or your sun sign, but you have other signs to consider, and they can direct what type of Sagittarius you are and how you present yourself to the world. There are sun signs, the most well-known among the Zodiac, moon signs, and rising signs or ascending signs.

The sun signs are the most known within western astrology, and when people refer to the Zodiac, they're referring specifically to sun signs. Most people only know their sun signs and haven't explored a Natal chart or birth chart, which reveals where their planets were in various houses during their birth. Most horoscopes you find online or receive through apps on your phone are only based on sun signs and don't account for other factors of your birth chart. This is often because of convenience. It is easy to calculate your sun sign because you only need to know your birthdate.

Sun signs play a key role in astrology and understanding the Zodiac for a few reasons. First, the Sun is the center of our solar system and is seen as the root of life. Second, as a planetary force it symbolizes the core self or ego. Finally, the Sun represents centeredness, life, and illumination. If you're looking to learn more about yourself, then you should learn about your sign.

Your sun sign is what you are; Sagittarius is the representation of core aspects of your identity that are unchangeable. Understanding this can help you become your best self by acknowledging and understanding common challenges while playing to your personality strengths. Those who focus on walking a path that aligns with their energy and their individual sign will often see greater successes in life and greater connection to planetary changes and vibrations.

Sagittarius as a Rising Sign or Ascendant

Rising signs are often called your ascendant, and this is how you present yourself to the world. Your chart begins with your rising sign, the first house of your chart. This will often unveil how you begin things in life and your alignment between spirit and body. Imagine if all the elements of your life were spanned across the sky. This is the horizon of that sky where the Sun rises.

It's unfortunate that people don't pay much attention to their rising or ascendant sign because it can help them understand how other people view them. While your sun sign is learning about yourself, your ascendant sign is learning about how you present yourself to others. When people find inconsistencies with their personality and their sun sign, their rising sign is often responsible.

For example, a Sagittarius born with their rising sign in Capricorn may initially appear reserved, hardworking, and quiet. Although Sagittarians are known for their ability to work diligently, they're rarely reserved or quiet. Most common is that the Sagittarius may initially seem shy or meek, and once they get to know the person or feel comfortable in the environment, their inner Sagittarians come out.

The ascendant sign changes depending on where you were born and the time of your birth. It is a bit more complicated than calculating your sun sign. Raising signs change every couple of hours, but you can find online calculators that can help you find your rising sign if you know the place and time of your birth.

Learning more about your rising sign gives you more self-awareness. You will better understand how you adapt to new surroundings and how that rising sign interacts with your sun sign. Rising signs do not inherently carry the same traits as sun signs. There are significant differences between both signs.

You will need to calculate or find an online calculator to find your ascending sign. To offer a bit of insight, here's a quick overview of Sagittarius ascending.

Sagittarius rising signs often rely heavily on intuition and are often found to be very confident with themselves in every situation. These are the people who will own every room they walk into, and if they don't know what's going on, they'll fake it. People with a Sagittarius rising sign are clever enough to get away with "faking it" through many situations and are very optimistic, which puts everyone else in a good mood.

Sagittarius as a Moon Sign

Your moon sign is an indicator of your inner self or the parts of yourself which you hide from other people, even those close to you. This is your innermost, emotional side, the areas of your personality you safeguard. Moon signs can also support the kind of parent you are, how you process emotions, and how you feel about your memories.

Lunar energy tends to manifest in different ways based on the element. For example, water moons are often extraordinarily empathetic and place a high value on emotion. Earth moons focus on creating stability in their finances and work life. Air and fire moons usually seek ways to cultivate their sun sign and to bring out their core personality without added responsibility.

A Sagittarius as a moon sign would drastically magnify the Sagittarian's drive for freedom. They may feel an extreme aversion to connecting to relationship ties or settling down. Those born with Sagittarius as their Moon sign are gypsy types with a need to wander and roam. They engage and emotions on two ends of the gamut. Moon Sagittarians desire alone time and independence to assess and evaluate their emotions. On the other end of the spectrum, moon Sagittarians seek new experiences and interactions with new people. They gain emotional benefits from watching other people process their feelings without having a relationship with that person.

Those with the moon in Sagittarius are also problem solvers. Because they look so critically at their inner self and separate themselves from relationships, they have a unique opportunity to analyze their feelings objectively.

Understanding Your Signs and How they Function Together

It's highly unlikely that you'll have Sagittarius as all three of your major signs. Before proceeding through the remaining chapters, you might quickly evaluate your natal chart online. Through an online chart creator, you can see your ascendant and moon sign. Those can both help you explore different areas of how you understand and express your core personality.

Get to know a bit about these other two signs. It can be very helpful to understand the elements of these signs and their ruling house. For example, anyone with a Cancerian moon sign might have greater receptivity to understanding emotions and processing emotions of those around them. This astrological superpower is because the moon is Cancer's ruling planet making it exceptionally strong. Just the same, a Leo ascendant radiates magnetic energy and pulls people toward them. They're self-aware and present their sun sign proudly because Leo is ruled under the Sun.

Then there's the matter of your signs working together, or often, against each other. A fire sign such as Sagittarius or Leo with a water sign Ascendant might seem shy, reserved, and laid back. A fire sign with a ground sign Ascendant might seem overly focused and headstrong.

Understanding how your various signs work together can navigate through your core self with greater confidence. If you know how you present yourself to others and how you process or hold on to emotions, you can identify how they fit into your individual personality. You can also use these factors within your whole personality to build a life that emphasizes your individual self's positive values and helps you overcome common challenges throughout life.

Chapter 3: Impact of Planetary Movements on a Sagittarius

Planetary movement or transits impact all our lives and mildly different ways. How the planets move is consistent for everyone. That is beyond our power, but how those movements impact us largely depends on our sun sign and how our houses appear on our natal chart. In the last chapter, we discussed the Natal chart or birth chart, and it's important in understanding astrology. There are a few takeaways you can grab from the planetary changes based on your sun sign alone. In this chapter, we will be looking at how these movements affect those born under the Sagittarius sign.

Remember that planetary bodies, which include Pluto, the sun, and the moon, are all in continuous motion. There's also the earth element, which means that understanding how these planets interact and move is a bit of a complex matter. As we work our way further away from the sun, we see larger orbits and fewer opportunities for these planets to enter your specific sign.

What Elements of the Universe Affect Sagittarius?

Virtually everything in the heavens can impact each person in a way consistent with their core personality or their sun signs. Planetary bodies within astrology include planets, stars, moons, and planetoids. Sometimes there is specific significance tied to certain signs where a planetoid or star may affect those signs and not others.

Sagittarius is one of these signs with Kaus Borealis and Kaus Australis found within its constellation. The presence of these two prominent stars can bring out key personality traits when their brightest and when Sagittarius is present. Kaus Borealis is associated with strength and flexibility, while Kaus Australia enhances goal setting and aiming high.

The impact of Sagittarius' stars will be greatest when Sagittarius is present. For those in the Northern Hemisphere, that is from early June to late August or early September.

Planetary Movements

The heavenly bodies and their movements are in constant flux; you can still use basic information about each body to plan ahead. Those who follow astrology may be familiar with terms like Mercury in retrograde, and this is where those terms come into action.

Astrologist's look years into the future to help map out when planets will enter certain houses and signs. This element of astrology is where it becomes more science than anything else. These planets and other celestial bodies move on predetermined tracks. These reliable movements caused ancient civilizations to use the movements of the planets and stars as the basis for their calendars and the calendars we use today.

Mercury in Sagittarius

Mercury appears in two primary formats. First, the planet can simply be in Sagittarius, or it can be in retrograde through Sagittarius. When Mercury interacts with Sagittarius, it promotes freedom of thought and open communication. The downside is that most of this communication starts quite optimistic and then takes a turn. Sagittarians should be especially careful to use whatever tech they have when they begin conversations because these discussions can quickly become arguments.

When Mercury is in Sagittarius, you may notice other signs taking on Sagittarius means of communicating. Other people may be less inclined to keep opinions to themselves or stay quiet about what they think during a conversation. Mercury is the house of communication, and it often prompts people to explore new ways to communicate. Unfortunately, so many people living mild amounts of fear of Mercury because of information problems.

There's another element that comes with Mercury being in Sagittarius. Organization. Sagittarians are never great at organization anyway, but they may feel the need to declutter when Sagittarius enters Mercury. For those born to Sagittarius, Mercury entering your sign often brings about the feeling of having too much stuff and the need for open space. It does, though your demand for personal freedom is manifesting in your immediate living space.

Mercury can remain in Sagittarius between 14 and 30 days. That doesn't offer a large window, but it does offer quick relief if that stretch of Mercury in Sagittarius isn't working out well.

Venus in Sagittarius

Venus is the planet of love and still rules relationships to this day. When Venus enters Sagittarius, people are more prone to see the good in each other. Other signs may put on those rose-colored glasses that Sagittarians wear daily. Additionally, Sagittarius natives and many other signs will perceive the need to learn new things about their partner and have new experiences together.

Venus can go on in Sagittarius for anywhere from 23 to about 60 days, and that can be *good news* for many relationships. Sagittarius natives feel the effect of Venus directly when it's in this sign. They may idolize their lover and appreciate their ideas and beliefs rather than engage in friendly debates and arguments. Sagittarians also become more serious when Venus is in their sign and may even consider settling down.

The great news is that when Venus is in Sagittarius, many people are generally more open to experiences and ideas. But if Venus is in Sagittarius for an extended amount of time, it may feel like an emotional overload. After about 20 days, Sagittarians are ready to move on from Venus, but they have a bit of a checklist. They typically aim to experience something new and build up their relationships before exiting Venus. Sagittarians should know that they don't demand to be perfect during this time. They can still be themselves and not overwhelm themselves with emotion. There isn't any desire to be perfect for their partner, parents, children, or friends. When in Venus, Sagittarius natives are easily pleased but can feel as though they're stuck in a rut or not contributing enough to their relationships.

Mars in Sagittarius

Mars is in Sagittarius for about one and a half months or six weeks. During that time, watch out. Sagittarians already have trouble keeping conversations from taking an unfortunate turn. When Mars is in Sagittarius, those born in Sagittarius have an exceptionally difficult time with patience, keeping their anger in control and restlessness during a conversation. Although Mars has nothing to do with communication, it has a lot to do with anger as the God of War rules it.

Sagittarians may offset a little of this by choosing text-based communication and taking measures to reduce the time spent waiting on a message. For example, instead of angrily waiting for your partner to text back while you're trying to cultivate an argument, turn your phone off for 10 minutes or leave it in the other room, forget about it for and then return to it. You might also try to set restrictions on your phone during work hours, or times you want to yourself so you won't be bothered with conversations that might distract you. Of course, this isn't a permanent solution. Sagittarians love social interaction, but sometimes for the sake of their friendships and other relationships, they might need to step back a little to avoid arguments and fights.

People with Mars in their Sagittarius on their natal chart do face peculiar issues for Sagittarians. If you are Sagittarius and Mars is in Sagittarius on your birth chart, you may have noticed a distinct problem with follow-through. Mars often embodies chaos, and when that mixes with the Sagittarian's gusto for life, it means big dreams and little action. If this is your case, carefully assess which projects you want to pursue and how much time you dedicate to that project. That way, you can reduce the number of half-done projects lying around the house or sitting on your desk.

Saturn in Sagittarius

Saturn and Sagittarius have quite a few things in common. They are both deeply entrenched in ethics, spirituality, and a higher mind, but Saturn and Sagittarius differ because Sagittarius is about restrictions and rules. Sagittarians, ruled under Jupiter, is about limitless possibilities and extraordinarily high aspirations. So, when Saturn enters Sagittarius and as it transits through, Sagittarians have this insane ability to carry out a lot of the projects they've started.

Sagittarians aren't known to set down a project, but they are known to take their time when Saturn is in Sagittarius. They have this acceptance period, where they acknowledge what they need to do and get it done. First Sagittarians, this is also a great opportunity to achieve a little inner reflection. Many Sagittarius natives use this time to evaluate how in tune they are with themselves and if they're giving their higher calling in life enough attention. It's an excuse to do a bit of moral inventory.

Uranus in Sagittarius

Uranus hasn't entered Sagittarius since 1988, and no one should expect it to circle around again anytime soon. When Uranus is in Sagittarius, there's a fair amount of rebellion. There are a lot of pushbacks against taboos, education, and belief systems. This is fairly consistent with what was experienced in the late 1980s and early 1990s. Uranus left Sagittarius in 1995.

The Ruling Planet of Sagittarius—Jupiter

Here is the planet that rules Sagittarius, Guardian to the abstract and higher mind, the yen for curiosity and ideas. There's really no way to downplay Jupiter. It's such a force.

Jupiter is the planet of luck, and promotes the formulation of ideology, operates within the spirit realm, and rules directly over religion and philosophy. These are all things that tie to the higher mind. That connection is what leads Sagittarians in their lifelong quest for learning and new experiences. It often leads many deep into the spiritual realm, and even when Sagittarians aren't necessarily religious, they may be interested in understanding religion and spirituality.

Let's explore that luck side for just a moment. We know that Jupiter is in your natal chart in the most important position, your sun sign. Jupiter has two streaks of luck. The first is plain luck. Good fortune just seems to come to them, and they often receive what they need at just the right moment. But there is also the stroke of the judge and jury element of luck. Sagittarians will often learn lessons the hard way when it feels like their good luck has run out, and then at the last moment, there could be leniency. Luck, at least with Jupiter, is not always about getting help when you need it. It can often simply be the lesser of other consequences.

Jupiter, in Roman mythology, was the God of both the Sky and nature. He was also called the father of both gods and men. In Greek mythology, this represents Zeus, who overthrew Saturn, or Kronos, father of Zeus. As part of this mythology, Jupiter serves as a bit of rebellion, but these stories mark the significance of ideology and religion as Zeus and Jupiter both overthrew gods who ruled through chaos and fear.

Mercury in Retrogrades Effect on Sagittarians

Mercury often retrogrades. On average, it will retrograde three or four times per year, and when it does, it brings trouble. Not all retrogrades are bad, but the impact of Mercury's stranglehold on communication often causes trouble for many signs. Sagittarius feels these impacts even more painfully than other signs because of their blunt way of communicating.

Although Sagittarians don't worry about what others think, especially if it's about something they said, this retrograde poses specific challenges. Sagittarians should expect to have frequent disagreements and feel constantly undermined in conversations when Mercury is in retrograde.

To counteract this, Sagittarius natives can focus not on the conversation itself but on the activity that comes from it. Especially at work, Sagittarians can focus on the affairs and good activity that happens because of other people sticking up for their opinions. Remember that your opinions and ideas often overwhelm those around you. The trouble is they see your passion as aggression, and they may not stand up to you to voice their own opinion. Most of the other signs don't realize that you're opinionated but also open-minded. Mercury in retrograde can be frustrating, but it can also present the opportunity you've wanted to get into deep and complex subjects with people who normally avoid conversation.

Sagittarius in Different Houses

There are 12 houses in the zodiac, and each houses a zodiac sign, but they are different. Instead, the house reflects the earth's reflection on its axis since the zodiac represents the movement of the earth around the sun. Of the 12 houses, it's common for people to have a closer tie to the house of their sun sign, but each house will affect your life.

When you have your birth chart or natal chart, you can find any planetary bodies in your different houses. This presents the opportunity to assess each facet of your personality and daily life, keeping the houses and planets in mind. This element sees both the trees and the forest; you're looking at the big picture with the small pieces in mind. The houses vary for each person as a small piece of their personality. Someone can have multiple planets or zero planetary bodies in any house, but you can use this quick guide to navigate the different houses through the Sagittarius personality's eyes.

1st House – House of First Impressions, Leadership, and Appearance – Ruled by Aries

The first house is ruled over by Aries and is larger than life. Sagittarians often feel deep within their first house, and that's where they get their sense of humor. Sagittarians with Sagittarius in their first house are certainly quick with smart remarks, but temper that off with a bit of goofy humor.

Even when Sagittarius is not in the first house, you strongly connect with leadership and first impressions. That can cause a strong connection.

2nd House–House of Environments, Senses, and Money–Ruled by Taurus

Sagittarians aren't always deeply rooted in their second house, it's ruled by the earth sign Taurus, and a lot of it has to do with travel. The difference between second house travel and Sagittarian travel is that Sagittarius natives have nomadic tendencies to learn and witness ideologies or spirituality in different countries. With the second house, this is the house of environments and senses, which often pulls more toward static environments.

3rd House–House of Communication, Travel, and Community–Ruled by Gemini

The third house is one of communication, travel, and community. When looking at your birth chart, consider how deeply connected you are to your community. Those with a fire sign in their third house will often feel a deeper understanding of obligation to those around them. If Sagittarius is in the third house, a person might feel torn between a need to get away and the need to stay.

What most Sagittarius get from their third house is a deep sense of community and communication. Sagittarius natives already have a solid foundation for travel, and they need not pull from another house to feed that need. Instead, this house can help Sagittarius understand how they interact with communities and how they communicate with strangers or people they've just met.

4th House–House of Home, Family, Privacy, and Foundation–Ruled by Cancer

This house represents home, family, and essentially starting a family of your own. It closely links to the moon, and your moon sign, and your sun sign, can play a part in your fourth house. The sign in your fourth house during your birth has the most monumental impact, and that is your moon sign. But, as different signs enter the fourth house, you'll feel subtle changes in your ideals around family and home.

5th House–House of Self-Expression, Creativity, Attention, and Fun–Ruled by Leo

The fifth house is about pleasure and satisfaction. Sagittarians often find great fun in travel or exploring other cultures. If you don't feel the wanderlust, then consider watching foreign sports teams, romance movies in different languages, or learning a new language yourself.

6th House–House of Health, Service, Routine, and Helpfulness–Ruled by Virgo

The sixth house is the house of health. Sagittarians notoriously have trouble with their hips and liver. They're prone to sciatica, but a Sagittarius may feel better as a few signs move through the sixth house. Of course, it's best to take responsibility for overall health. Stars or no stars, stay active, cultivate healthy routines, and maintain good diet habits.

7th House–House of Relationships, Both Business and Personal–Ruled by Libra

Libra sees over the seventh house, but as different signs move through it, there are fluctuations in daily events regarding relationships. The seventh house is largely responsible for personal and business, but it's typically called the house of marriage.

8th House–House of Birth, Death, Transformation, and Energy–Ruled by Scorpio

The house of birth and death often feeds carnal desires such as energy and sex, but it can also manifest in hatred and anger. If you're harboring anger, then watch out as Sagittarius enters the eight house. When you're watching your star chart, pay careful attention to this house, it's a great opportunity to approach sex, and redefine your energy.

9th House–House of the Higher Mind, Religion, and Education–Ruled by Sagittarius

This is your house, the house of the higher mind and education. Explore and learn everything you can as long as it's fun and engaging. If something becomes "work" and not mandatory to your career path, drop it. Your ninth house can help you build a great wealth of knowledge if it doesn't weigh you down. This will heavily affect your career.

10th House-House of Structure, Tradition, Career, and Image-Ruled by Capricorn

This house is how we feel about the rest of the world. It brings us to assess and accept our obligations, plan out for big projects, and to know when to accept personal responsibility. Capricorn is largely a responsible and organized sign, so not surprisingly, this is its house, but the overwhelming trouble is that Sagittarians have almost a natural allergy to planning and feel compelled to follow obligations. It's likely that you'll struggle to identify with this house throughout your life.

11th House-House of Friendships, Technology, and Future-Ruled by Aquarius

Sagittarius natives know all about friendship and often have the most tumultuous and rewarding experiences in friendship, but this house also rules over technology and what lays ahead. Any Sagittarian may feel a strong pull toward the changes that the eleventh house brings.

12th House-House of Endings, Tying Loose Ends, and the Afterlife-Ruled by Pisces

The twelfth house is reasonably the house of endings and the one that can also result in undoing. Sagittarius people need to be exceptionally careful and aware of their twelfth house as it can lead to a fair amount of self-sabotage. This drives people into secret affairs to destroy a stable and loving relationship. Or where you might continually put off a big work project because it's easier to fail and risk getting fired than to face the challenge of moving up.

All these houses impact your daily life, and with an active star chart, you can plot exactly which houses you must face with the most attention on any day.

Chapter 4: Strengths of Sagittarians

Sagittarian natives have unique superpowers in the world of the zodiac. They see the good, the light, and act with the assumption that the best is yet to come. Manifesting and working towards the positive outcomes are what set Sagittarians apart from the rest of the signs and leads to all their strengths. They're often applauded as the best-natured of the fire signs and most fun-loving of the entire zodiac.

Those born under Sagittarius love life and are optimistic about all the wonderful things to come. They see no point in dwelling over the past or obsessing over things that might go wrong. Sagittarius' natives fixate on the intangible word in those situations. They see the "might" and "possibly" and the "could" as unlikely events they shouldn't worry about. Typically, Sagittarians don't focus on their misfortunes either, often because they know that good luck or a turn for the better is near.

Their ability to look toward the future enables them to play towards the strengths regularly. We're going to cover weaknesses and common Sagittarian challenges in the next chapter, but you'll see here that it's often a matter of these challenges being of a similar nature to their strengths. When a Sagittarian goes overboard, there can be a few drawbacks. But, for now, we'll focus on how these strengths often allow Sagittarius natives to live their best lives with generally little effort.

As the cherry on top, Sagittarius natives tend to have the most direct and straightforward personalities, which make them focused on their strengths. They don't prefer to get muddled by all the other little things in life. Most of the time, Sagittarians find out what they're good at and spend their lives improving in those areas or using those strengths to learn and explore other areas of life.

Loyalty

Loyalty is a frequent presence among fire signs. Unlike other elements, fire signs are most notably loyal. Although Sagittarians are free spirits and don't like getting trapped into a clique, they'll still be devoted to various people in their lives.

The usual or typical setup for this style of loyalty in a Sagittarius' life is that they'll often connect with a few friends scattered across a few different friend groups. Using standard high school cliques as an example, a Sagittarius might have one close jock friend, another close preppy friend, and another close punk friend. None of these friends independently will understand how they all came to be friends with the Sagittarius or why they all found such good friends in one person, but Sagittarius' can often bring unexpected people together, and when that happens, it's magical. They not only deliver outstanding loyalty, but they cultivate it in other people.

One character example Sagittarian is Rachel Green from Friends. A Sagittarian who clearly is the glue among the oddball assortment of companions in the group. They don't find themselves in cliques, but instead are found giving their loyalty to independent friends, or extracting the best from each clique to build a group of friends.

Sagittarians also hate prejudices, and they actively work to cultivate friends from all backgrounds. They want to be friends with the world, but they know that it can lead to trouble. As Sagittarius natives make friends easily, it can seem as though they'd have problems devoting their loyalties to only a few people. That couldn't be further from the case. A Sagittarius native might find this easy, but they only have a handful of best friends. In that sense, they offer unmatched loyalty, and they can easily rank their loyalty to specific friends.

If you are a friend, family member, or romantic partner to a Sagittarius, you may have witnessed this loyalty firsthand. Those who put ultimatums to Sagittarius born people such as, "it's them or me" the person proposing the ultimatum will lose. If they ask them to choose between their relationship or their friends, the friends will win.

As a friend to a Sagittarius, you're lucky beyond belief. But be careful not to ask too much from your Sagittarian friend because they're loyal and generous enough to give more than they can.

As a family member to a Sagittarian, tread carefully. Sagittarius born are loyal, but unlike Cancer, Leo, or Pisces, they don't inherently value family members above friends. Aim to cultivate a friendship as they enter adulthood and accommodate their needs as best you can without groveling for their friendship. Sagittarians hate groveling.

As a Sagittarian's romantic partner, there's much opportunity for lifelong loyalty, but also the risk of losing it all quickly. Sagittarians are notoriously hard to pin down, so if you're in a relationship, you've cleared the biggest hurdle. But, if it ever becomes a matter between you and the others in their life, they'll likely choose those who they've known for years over a lover.

Sagittarians are supportive of those individuals in their life, and they want to see them succeed. They also prefer to see people in good relationships and to cultivate relationships and friendships that stand the test of time.

Where a Sagittarius can falter in this strength is sentimentality. There's one overwhelming element in Sagittarius: they speak their mind. They are the friend who will always be honest and forthcoming. Unfortunately, many people can't handle that, and they will often leave. That's okay, though, because Sagittarius natives don't enjoy the sentimentality of fragile or overly emotional people. They don't give their loyalty in exchange for anything. It's free. They only expect to not be taken advantage of, used, or exploited.

Naturally Athletic and Adventurous

Sagittarians are athletes, whether they particularly aim towards athletic excellence or not. Their athletic nature helps to build up their adventurous strength. Sagittarius want to get out into the world; walking through the many wonders and traveling deep into foreign countries or new towns. Typically, Sagittarians take long strides and swing their arms when they walk. It's very purposeful.

And they might enjoy athletic activities that deliver a thrill, things like spelunking, mountain climbing, bike riding, CrossFit, or even yoga. If it can take you to new places or deliver unique experiences, then it's worth the Sagittarian's time.

The strength lies in the fact that this culminates in a larger collection of planetary impact. First, you have the ruling planet Jupiter, God of Gods. Second, you have the energy and passion of the Fire element and finally, you have the change accepting factor of the modality. They exude a vitality for life, and they spread it. They energize other people with this strong internal energy.

The best way to keep up this strength is to do more of it. Exercise, explore, or be active often in life. When you're taking a break at work, take a walk around the building or the area. Even if it's only to the parking lot and back, it will boost your energy for the rest of the day. Better yet, you'll likely find that many people will go with you. People naturally prefer to be around you, especially when you're active. That's because they unknowingly have a magnetic attraction to your high level of adventure and athleticism, and they want to share in that vitality for life.

Sagittarius natives must know they shouldn't be shut in for too long. You might need to get out of the house or the office building, so you don't feel closed in and separated from this natural strength of yours. Better yet, you may pursue a career or hobby that enables you to build on these strengths regularly.

Curious

Curiosity killed the cat, but the Archer is safe in this scenario. Sagittarians often let their curiosity lead them through life. They are the toddler or child who constantly asks, "What's this?" or "Why?" and they want full answers. This reigns because of Jupiter. As the planet of higher mind that Sagittarians have a natural pull toward learning.

But Sagittarius natives will reach a point where they have the control to direct their curiosity. As children, Sagittarians show interest in everything from art to math and even deep into music and the outdoors. They're the children that are extremely demanding when it comes to their parents having enough energy to keep up. But, as they reach their mid or late-twenties, they know what they're generally good at and can direct their curiosity toward that field and related subjects.

For example, two famous Sagittarius authors include Mark Twain and C. S. Lewis. Although both wrote extensively in fiction, both also explored multiple genres and wrote observational non-fiction for the time's politics and ethics. They used their skill in writing to explore other interests they held. It's also worth noting here that these two Sagittarians were extremely strong in the pursuit of knowledge. Although only C. S. Lewis received a formal education, Mark Twain was a passionate lifelong learner. Twain used his love of language and printed material to explore other elements that weren't taught in school. While working at a printing press, he used that time and access to materials to learn about botany, history, and government.

Positive to a Fault

In the opening of this chapter, we couldn't get enough of Sagittarian's positive attitude, and it's true. You probably won't find a more positive person in life than a Sagittarius. They're also willing to spread that positivity.

The result of this high level of positivity is often a great sense of humor, willingness to crack a joke, and an extroverted personality. They're extremely direct people and spend little time worrying about the possible consequences of their behavior.

In the best of times, this means that the Sagittarian can devote plenty of time to manifesting their best life. They walk into situations believing that the best outcome isn't just possible. It's the most likely outcome. They're happy, and simply being happy often drives many people to treat them well, and give them what they want. Sagittarians also, unintentionally, provoke a lot of romantic relationships with this positivity.

All of this comes from fire's radiant energy and Jupiter's innate luck. They bring their own light into the world, and they don't rely on anybody else for their happiness. With eccentric optimism, they tend towards impatience and be a little too easy to excite. As children, they can be demanding and occasionally annoying because of their high energy, while as adults, they might seem self-centered or too energetic for many people. That's fine because, again, Sagittarius natives don't need anyone else to be happy; so as far as they're concerned, this is not their problem.

Independent

Sagittarians value independence highly; they hold on to it with a vice grip. They want the opportunity to release their passions, seek all the knowledge of the universe, and live with reckless abandon. Looking for independence and unquestioned freedom.

This seems like a weakness to everyone else, as though they can't be tied down and never have meaningful roots in any specific place or with any person. But the Sagittarius would never be bothered or influenced by other people. The Capricorn-Sagittarius cusp may exude this to an even higher degree.

They are also very straightforward, and with the cusps of this sign, that can easily mean a lot of angry outbursts, but Sagittarians are usually laid back, and understanding Scorpios and Capricorns are not.

How is this a strength for Sagittarius natives? Their high level of independence gives them the freedom to seek whatever they want from life. These people think far outside of the box and are exceptionally skilled with creative problem solvers because they aren't tied to other people. And they handle internal struggles easily because they've learned early in life they need not rely on anyone else.

Understanding the Overall Personality of the Strong Sagittarian

As a whole, few things seem like contradictions but work together to create such a strong force behind their personality strengths.

First, they are both loyal and independent. But most of the time, people confuse the two as the opposite when they're just different. Sagittarians don't rely on other people for anything, and that means they can give a different loyalty than what most people experience from other signs. They want nothing for their loyalty, and they may seem like a distanced friend, but true friends of a Sagittarius native know how important their independence is to them.

Second, they are hyper curious and athletic. People have adopted this "brains or brawn" mentality, and it looks like a person can't be both. That's evidently not true, and not every Sagittarius is brawny per se, but enjoys adventure. Usually, adventure requires physical prowess, but many Sagittarians have found another way to create adventure. C. S. Lewis, the creator of The Chronicles of Narnia and much other fantasy and Sci-Fi novels, cultivated his own adventures. He didn't need to venture out into the wilderness; he made his own world with his curiosity and his intellect.

Finally, a Sagittarius may seem blunt, brazen, and oddly... exceptionally positive. It seems like bluntness and insensitivity would seem like a negative person's trait, but these all come from a positive person. They will say what they want with little regard for anyone else because of their high value for independence, but their positivity often means this is coming from a good place. If a Sagittarian says, "Your diet can't be going too well if you keep inviting me out for pizza," they aren't saying that the other person is fat. They're pointing out that their friend isn't meeting the expectations that they set for themselves. This Sagittarius is offering support through the only way they know-how; they don't doubt they can meet their goals – *they're just trying to help reach the standard they want to achieve.*

Overall, Sagittarians are something different. They can seem like a bonkers assortment of personalities, but they have it together, and when they don't, it doesn't bother them.

Chapter 5: Common Sagittarius Challenges

Sagittarians may ride their independently created high for most of their life, but everyone faces challenges. While they are ruled under Jupiter, which has a huge role in their life, and it's the largest body in the solar system besides the sun, they always are on the cusp of excellence and expansion. These are the people who explore and want to know absolutely everything about the world around them. That is where they experience most of their challenges.

If you've lived around a Sagittarius, you might have noticed these demands tie directly into their core personality, and sometimes they don't even notice. For Sagittarius natives, reading through these challenges may be truly eye-opening. Unlike other facets of the Zodiac, those well-versed in planetary movement and the sun signs, this won't be a moment where you can sit back and nod your head in agreement. Many Sagittarians may outright argue that these aren't challenges. Many could even push that they're positive elements of their personality!

Those who know a Sagittarius native will easily see these challenges or weaknesses common among those born to the ninth house.

Impatience

A Sagittarius native cannot and will not wait patiently for anything. Sagittarians are among the children of the Zodiac and embody this style of forever-young mental state. This stems directly from their modality and their wish for ultimate flexibility and constant movement, but that need for constant movement is the same thing as outright restlessness.

The mutable element encouraged them to accept change and seek constant change. In an instance where a Sagittarius may be told to wait six months for a promotion, that person is more likely to leave their job and to find a different position with another company. Even if that doesn't result in a promotion, it's something different, and Sagittarians crave that.

In terms of school, many Sagittarians are checked out by the time they hit high school. They may manage this in one of two ways. They may see high school as a necessary evil and simply do enough to get by and rebel completely. Or, they will excel and stay among the top of their class to have the most options available to them after graduation. Sagittarians are big goal-oriented, and others of them can think of their long game, but many tend to focus on the short game and can't be patient enough to reap the full rewards of their hard work.

In the workforce, the Sagittarian's need for change usually leads to impatience, and that impatience is worn right on their sleeve. A Sagittarius won't appreciate being stuck in a dead-end position, and they won't like being overly committed to a company. They may even quit a job to prove how much freedom they have.

With love, the need to change and move forward rarely drives them in the direction that people would expect. They don't rush into marriage, and they are not impatient to settle down and start a family. If anything, they are impatient to reignite that steamy romance that fuels the beginning of a relationship. They love the honeymoon phase, and for them, the need for change is rushing toward that honeymoon phase again, even with a new person.

Intolerance

Two primary factors contribute to this weakness, and this is one challenge that Sagittarians might count as a superpower period. But watch out because they may be falling for their own foolishness. Sagittarians receive a gift from the ruling planet Jupiter and the 9th house being the higher mind's house. Sagittarians can read people and assess deeper elements of a person at face value.

Arrange their exceptionally intuitive nature allows them to pick up on a person's character quickly. On its own, it is a gift, but when you combine that with their overwhelming honesty and their want to have an entire society of non-conformists, Sagittarians simply can't stand individuals who wear a mask in public. If a Sagittarius can tell that someone is different in private than they are when around other people, they will reject them from their lives. These are not people to be polite for the sake of being polite. They don't deal out "BS", or put up with it either.

There are two other personality factors that Sagittarians absolutely cannot stand. A Sagittarius native will not tolerate someone being selfish. This is where Sagittarians do differ from other fire signs. Although both generous, Aries and Leo put their needs above the needs of others. They would weigh out both sets of needs separately and decide which was the most logical course of action before simply putting their demands first.

Afraid of Commitment

This issue is not necessarily a weakness or a downfall, but is instead a matter of misinterpretation. It's a challenge that Sagittarians experience because of what everyone else thinks. But Sagittarius natives don't care what anyone else thinks, or their level or ability to commit. They realize that they're freedom seekers, and that they won't be forced into any relationship.

Sagittarians often view romantic situations in a negative light as a situation of one adult controlling or holding back another adult. That's not the case, and it can take Sagittarians a lifetime to figure out that good relationships don't involve anyone controlling or manipulating the other person.

Now, Sagittarius natives don't like feeling fenced in, and relationships can certainly cause that, but they aren't afraid to commit. They fear committing to the wrong person. A Sagittarius will rarely give this much consideration to the possibility of something going wrong. They are naturally positive people and don't think about things going wrong, but with relationships, they will spend a lot of time dwelling on all the things that could work out the wrong way.

To put it simply, if someone shows even the slightest inclination of:

- Complicated drama (including family drama)
- Perpetual selfishness
- Need for constant approval
- Judgmental nature

A Sagittarian native truly craves that deep soulmate connection, but they know that it's a once-in-a-lifetime shot. They aren't in any hurry to rush into a relationship or a commitment with anyone who might not fit the bill. Instead, they're likely to have many relationships while on the search for someone that will help bring out the best in them so they can return the favor.

Sagittarians need someone who can keep up with their high energy or enjoy sitting out occasionally. Letting the Sagittarius native have freedom is important, and they typically believe that freedom and independence should foster the relationships even during marriage.

One of the primary challenges that a Sagittarius will experience is that others feel they're afraid of commitment. Others will try to push the Sagittarius native to commit or move on and become impatient, which can mean they experience the end of many relationships. This challenge is that they will believe it is a "not my problem" situation, but if they don't communicate what they expect from the relationship, it will quickly become their problem.

Bluntness

With communication, Sagittarians don't hesitate to "tell it like it is." They say exactly what they mean, and they say it whenever they feel like letting the words loose into the world. Overall, it's an utter lack of discipline and tact, but they're just speaking the truth from the Sagittarian viewpoint, and everyone deserves to hear it.

This particular challenge comes up whenever they are unhappy. You may notice in many other sun signs that people might clam up, retreat, or silently brew over words they want to say but know aren't right. A Sagittarius just won't do that, and it comes down to the factors of their ruling planet Jupiter and their fire element. These two combined mean they are passionately on the quest for truth and knowledge and want everyone else to experience it. When the Sagittarius native is hurt, they'll take to very public forums to ensure that everyone knows how they were wronged and what they think about it.

In the workplace, this causes significant issues and challenges. A Sagittarian may struggle to move up within a company or stay on any team for very long, not only because they lack patience but also because they just have no tact. It's likely that someone in the company or on the team will get tired of listening to the Sagittarius complaining about the same thing or worse, dropping "truth bombs" in important meets or emails.

For Sagittarians, you might try a few of these tactics to overcome this struggle:

- Practice active listening where it may be inappropriate to voice an opinion. For example, when another person is leading a meeting.

- Don't address large groups on matters which involve specific individuals. For example, don't respond to the entire company in an email when the matter involves only one or two people.

- When feeling like you need to educate those around you on how things "really are", give yourself a break and step away. Your fire side may spur a craze of anger and leave everyone feeling bad about the situation.

Careless and Often Bored

It would be a grave mistake to say that a famous Sagittarian such as Winston Churchill was careless, but he certainly had his moments and was often bored. In fact, he was notorious for walking away from things that didn't keep his attention or wouldn't result in action. He had no time for people who were all talk, and when he grew bored with something, he let others handle it. For carelessness, there are key moments in history that mark this leader's often forgotten challenge. The Great Fog incident in which many people died because of the government not taking measures to protect the people is possibly the most notable. Churchill brushed off this danger as "mere fog" and could not be bothered to give it any more attention.

Sagittarians want to live a happy life and to do that. They put all their focus on the present. That is why many great leaders are the great leaders we know them as they looked at the present and made the best possible decisions for the time, but daily, this can present problems.

They may leave multiple projects unfinished for long periods and be inconsistent for handling elements within their work life. Anytime there's a matter involving someone counting on them, they might have trouble keeping tabs on why something is important when it is also boring.

To avoid boredom:

> • Connect regularly with those who value the task as critical or vital for frequent reminders of why these boring tasks are necessary.

> • Devote a limited amount of time to boring tasks, so it is manageable and does not overtake your life.

> • Determine how much time it is fair to give to boring projects or tasks, so they don't feel like they are taking forever.

To avoid carelessness:

> • Ask a friend or coworker to go over your work.

> • Create a checklist at the beginning of the task when you're still very focused and then use it at when you are close to completion of the task to make sure you didn't cut corners.

> • Enjoy the learning process; focus on what you're experiencing and learning rather than how much you want the project closed.

To help a Sagittarian overcome this challenge:

> • Create extrinsic rewards for milestone completions.

> • Offer the ability to learn and investigate new factors of the project or task whenever possible.

> • Take advantage of their bluntness to determine when a task or milestone isn't necessary or doesn't serve a purpose.

Special Challenges for Cusps

As mentioned before, many Sagittarius natives fall right on the cusp lines for Scorpio or Capricorn, and these two signs often aren't reasonable or easy-to-handle cusps. Scorpio comes with a slew of complications in communication, emotion processing, and the opposing planet's matter. Where a Sagittarius always looks to the future and thrives for positivity, Scorpio is quite the contrary.

Scorpio-Sagittarius Cusp

Battle of emotions, the Sagittarius with their big emotions and the Scorpio that hides their emotions under a thick shell, is a recipe for explosive arguments after long brooding periods. They're also more prone to feel unappreciated and not say anything. They may work through long periods of boring work with no reward and feel slighted or disengaged with nothing else to show for it. They will hate this and often take it out on their loved ones instead of those in their workplace.

These cusps should speak up more and take responsibility for putting their complaints with the right person. Seek someone that can help your situation rather than those around you.

Sagittarius-Capricorn Cusp

With Capricorns, there's the matter of both the Capricorn and Sagittarian side loving others to be wrong. Now, from the Sagittarius point, they love to debate and learn and argue. They don't want the other person to feel wrong. They just want to win the argument while Capricorn wants to make someone feel like they never might win an argument against them when they're mad.

Sagittarius-Capricorn cusps should pay careful attention to how they speak to people. These communication downfalls can cause a lot of lost friendships so important to Sagittarians.

Chapter 6: Sagittarius Through Childhood

Sagittarians are among those within the forever children of the zodiac. They would be the lost boys of Neverland, as they simply don't seem to get older, but their childhood experiences will dramatically shape the adult Sagittarian, more so than other signs. For example, a Sagittarius who received a lot of praise as a child will probably seek a rewarding career with frequent praise. Although Sagittarians don't exceptionally care for what others think, they will associate that frequent praise with the comfort of home.

But there is a more common situation that Sagittarians face. Hating their childhood, or having an extreme dislike for it. One of the primary weaknesses of a Sagittarius is their inability to deal with certain types of people. Suppose they grew up with someone they saw as extremely needy or someone who seemed to victimize themselves perpetually. There, they would likely have an even harder time being around those who do this later in life. They may forsake their family, even though they are exceptionally loyal.

The wrongs and good deeds that Sagittarians experienced as children will act as their north star throughout life. They will use it to guide themselves toward what they believe is best for themselves and help to expose how they can improve and learn from their early childhood experiences.

What to Expect from Sagittarian Children

A Sagittarius child will display at high levels of activity almost around the Clock. Expect these children to stop taking naps early into their toddler years, and waver between independent and needy. Sagittarius child is exploring their need for freedom, but they want to do so with the safety net. They may attach more to one parent than the other at various points, and that could be to test the waters of what each parent will let them get away with doing.

A Sagittarius child might be very happy playing on their own or with siblings through the early years, but it's not likely that they will form a very strong bond with the siblings unless they are close in age. During the toddler years, they may be easy to help reach milestones. Sagittarius children typically learn toilet training faster, are more helpful with household chores, and take pride in completing a project, whether that is for preschool or an art project of their own creation. These are all factors of their budding personality. They are valuable in home, and they pick up on these early age milestones so quickly because they already foster that need for independence—their wish to participate in projects and play with groups fuels their growing extraversion.

It is possible during childhood that Sagittarians males and females differ the most. Women will spend this time exploring different facets of their identity, and by the time they reach their teenage years, they'll have most of their core personality solidified and ready for adulthood. Sagittarian males use early childhood as playtime and then figure out their identity during their teen years and eventually solidify into their core in their 20s or even 30s.

Sagittarius Girls

Sagittarius girls are a pleasure to raise. They have extraordinarily disarming charms about them. They use their inquisitive nature to prompt others into engaging with them on a deeper level than most children can prompt from an adult. They're also quick to let any thoughts they have rush out of their mouth, which makes for a complete lifetime of "Kids Say the Darndest Things."

They startle and surprise most people with their intellect, their curiosity, in their bluntness. These are the kids who ask where babies come from at a very young age, and they're the ones who will ask why it's essential to get good grades or why it's necessary to want to be something when they become adults. And they want real answers. They won't take fluffy answers. They will keep digging until an adult gives them a quantifiable answer they can sit right with.

Unfortunately, a lot of parents of Sagittarius girls will frequently apologize for the things their child says. These parents should also be careful not to say anything they don't want repeated. You would not want to joke about the desire to kick a (mean) family dog in front of the young Sagittarius girl, who will find her aunt and report the statement promptly.

You see, Sagittarius girls are always listening. They need to know exactly who is around them, and who supports them into adulthood. They will quickly form very strong bonds with the people in their family they feel are most suitable for raising them. These young girls may attach to an aunt or cousin with more devotion than they would to their siblings.

But Sagittarian girls come out with one of the most redeeming qualities in children. They are hopelessly devoted to the truth, and you should never expect your Sagittarius native little girl to lie. These young children are also optimistic. The Sagittarius girls are a bit more suspicious about the ebb and flow of life than Sagittarius males are, but you'll notice that most Sagittarius girls persevere through life with a can-do attitude.

Sagittarius Boys

Sagittarius boys will give anyone a run for their money. These boys need to be born to another high strung fire sign that can keep up with their energy. When Aries or Leos have Sagittarian boys, they can thrive together and cultivate a lifelong relationship that naturally progresses is from parent to child to an adult friendship based on mutual respect.

These little boys are at venturers. They need to get outside and play in the dirt and not come in until the sun is down. If they are prone to video games, then they want adventure-based games with lots of action and big worlds to explore. Sagittarius boys show many of the most prominent challenges in their early years. These boys will outright rebel against any sign of routine, and they will outright hate normalcy.

As toddlers, this can be extremely difficult for any parent; what almost makes it worse is that the young boy is simply having fun, and hopefully, the parent can show they shouldn't shut that down every time. Yes, sometimes, you do need to adhere to a schedule or meet certain milestones but parents of Sagittarius boys should remember that they are very young children, and especially as toddlers, playtime is often more important than following a schedule or routine. This child uses playtime to explore the world around them and better understand how the surrounding adults are acting.

Although Sagittarius girls may be much more mature than boys in childhood, one thing that boys do is to *reenact through imagination.* Through imaginative play, you may notice that Sagittarius boys will often act out things that seem far out of the realm of normal, but they're exploring conversation and deep concepts. They may be playing Pirates, but what they're doing is exploring the idea of right and wrong, theft and redemption, slang, and formal speech.

One of the biggest differences between Sagittarius natives in their younger years is that boys are a bit more charming. Sagittarius girls will use their bluntness and curiosity to spurn adults into specific behavior, while boys are sweet and welcoming. They want to be around you, and they don't want your undivided attention. They simply want your presence. Most boys won't begin to explore that wish for freedom until their teenage years. They might also reserve more their curiosity until they're teenagers.

Early Social Butterflies

Even at young ages, Sagittarians are just social butterflies. They can't help but make acquaintances, and their high energy is perfect for leading childhood games.

Even as babies, they might enjoy being held by a multitude of people, not just their parents. When they enter toddler years, they relate to others with ease and find friends in almost any environment. They are the kid who happily waves bye to mom or dad as they run off into the preschool room while other kids are crying that their parents are leaving.

Parents of Sagittarius natives might have to work a little harder to instill the idea of "stranger danger" - or untrustworthy people. They need to prove who has certain responsibilities with them and when things are or are not right. For example, if parents are separated, you may work to explain who will pick them up after school or which bus they should be taking home. There is also a high risk of carelessness when it comes to social situations. A Sagittarius child may not be aware of how late it has gotten or that their friends have moved on to something else or another activity.

Require Constant Entertainment

One element of a common struggle for Sagittarians children is that they need constant entertainment and stimulation until they learn to engage in imaginative play at about the ages of four to six. They need someone to walk them through how to play with certain toys and how to engage with other children. Although Sagittarius children make fast friends, they desire someone to show them how to participate in that play at an early age.

Sagittarius kids do love exploring the world and will happily bring you a mountain of rocks, sticks, or acorns they collect or turn into projects. They prefer to do these things with someone, they don't want to be sent out into the backyard alone, and the parent will quickly be notified about their opinion on that situation.

There are a few challenges with entertaining young Sagittarians in a public space. Sagittarius natives love the hustle and bustle, but taking a Sagittarius child into a grocery store or out for a shopping trip may seem like a chore because they want to get into everything. From pulling things off shelves to loading up the cart with random items, they will find ways to stay entertained if the adult in the situation isn't providing them an outlet.

Now, if you have a child like this, you can make this game. Remember that Sagittarians love the idea of responsibility even at a young age, and they understand that it helps foster their independence in later years. Even as a toddler, they can help pick out items off the shelf and dutifully placed them in the cart. Make sure that if you're taking them out for an errand, you give them a job and make them feel like they're an important part of the task at hand.

Understanding Your Childhood

Now, this is not inherently a Sagittarius problem. Many people struggle to understand their childhood and the lens that crafted their view of the world. As this sign you might feel drawn to this troublesome issue because of your connection to the planet of the higher mind and your deep-set curiosity.

Perhaps the first step is to review your parent's actions with a little of compassion. Sagittarius natives are quick to evaluate people in a harsh light and make judgments they stick with for long periods of time. As an adult, you might consider that your parents were in a much different situation than you understood as a teenager or as a child. Even just by reading this chapter, you could notice certain patterns that your caregivers had to struggle with as you developed your independence and your personality.

High-energy children often report they did not feel as though they had enough attention or engagement as a young child. Now, if the parent in the picture was also working full time, then it's likely that the Sagittarius child spent more time in school or with babysitters. As an adult, you can understand a lot more about the situation surrounding your childhood, but that doesn't explain away your feelings.

As a fire sign, you have a tendency to be more logical in how you view the world, even with those Sagittarius rose-colored glasses giving you that optimistic framing. This would be the moment to assess your childhood analytically and see what positives you could take away from the experience. Many Sagittarius natives don't feel a deep connection to their family, even if they have loyalty towards them. Allow yourself to consider the factors around your childhood and explore what may have happened that was beyond your reach.

What a Sagittarius Child Needs

Now, a Sagittarius child demands a lot. They need a great deal of attention, creative outlets, engagement and energy; but when a parent can deliver this, it's an exceptional experience. These are the children who will ask questions that make you smile and generally make observations that seem like they come from an adult's mind.

They are ready and happy to learn about the world around them, and they already have an optimistic view of life. Even at early toddler ages, they often think in the frame of the best-case scenario is likely to happen.

The parent to a child of this sign should not expect the child to sit for long periods of time or undergo confinement in playpens. It may initially seem that the Sagittarius child is impatient and high energy; when the adult tries to engage them and run out that energy, they can compromise and set up routines if they understand that their needs are met through those routines.

Chapter 7: Sagittarians, "The Best Friend"

The ninth sign of the zodiac combines personality traits that prime them for a best friend position in nearly anyone's circle. They're extraordinarily open-minded, and they tend to surround themselves with diverse individuals. They will generally bring an eclectic collection of acquaintances that could thrive together, depending on their signs and aspects of their personality. They are looking for the widest variety of people possible, and it's easy to think that they might have a checklist of sorts for keeping friends around.

Sagittarians are always on the lookout for the chance of meeting new individuals. It's not just that they're outgoing. They're genuinely interested in learning about various life experiences. They're out for the opportunity to hear about other ways of going through life and assessing relationships and personality elements. A Sagittarian will rarely pass up the excuse to sincerely converse with someone about their opinions, views, or experiences. Sagittarius natives make friends extraordinarily fast, and often the other person feels as though they've made a friend for life, but that is for them to decide.

Although Sagittarians make friends quickly, they usually only have a small circle of people they consider close. Within that circle, they are the truest form of their "self" and it's when they're with their friends that they're happiest. If you're the trusted close friend of a Sagittarian, then you have something truly special, and you should be sure to feed or bolster that friendship frequently.

Friends of Sagittarians and the Sagittarius native themselves have difficulty with maintaining relationships. While they are always approachable, they have trouble feeling trapped or overly committed. It may seem like they've made a new best friend only to drop them or move on to another person a few weeks or months later.

As an overview of the Sagittarius as a friend, they are open, sincere, loving, and loyal. They will genuinely show interest in their friend's drama and anything they have to say, making nearly every other sign feel good about themselves. Fire signs most notably have a deep connection to character and self. As the last fire sign, Sagittarians love helping others boost their ego while getting a little surge of ego themselves.

Who is Sagittarius as a Friend?

A Sagittarius is the best of friends, they're the life of the party, and they're the ones who always want to have a bit of fun. To give a few pop culture references, Aang from Avatar: The Last Airbender, Gina from Brooklyn Nine-Nine, and Penny from The Big Bang Theory are all Sagittarians and fierce friends. The other element of this friendship you can easily see in these examples is how they are all unapologetically themselves around each other. That is one trait in a friendship that makes them such good people and draws others in so closely.

Sagittarians will rarely put on a mask for anyone. They don't need to impress society or anyone individually, but this isn't an *"I do what I want to stick it to everyone else"* issue. They genuinely don't think that what anyone else thinks matters. Jupiter rules over this sign, and through the many mythological tales of Jupiter or Zeus, they just have no one to impress. They are the God of Gods and the defeater of

Gods. This ties into the relationship because this raw authenticity is something that nearly every other person in existence envies or desires to achieve. So many people live behind masks or do things to appease others, and when they see Sagittarians not even considering that as an option, they want in on it. They want to experience that love of self and life in the raw how Sagittarians do; it is through friendship that happens.

Now, Sagittarians love a good party, and that doesn't align with everyone. For enough people, it hits home, and a Sagittarius isn't always looking for the house-rocking, party-hopping, have-the-cops-called-for-being-too-loud type of party. Sometimes they're truly happy at a small kickback or backyard bar-b-que. They bring to each gathering, no matter how big or small, their raw and uncontainable personality and energy.

As a friend, you can count on this sign to connect people and with people. Will you spend a lot of time alone with them? Probably not. Those under this sign are a few of the most extroverted that you may ever meet, and unlike other hot and fiery signs like Leos, they want little solitary time to recharge. Unlike Aries, they don't get overly aggressive and need to waste time putting the pieces of every relationship back together every couple of weeks. Now, a Sagittarius can have a bad day or streak where they're too blunt, too forthcoming with their opinions, and too "in everyone's business", but that's usually to blame on a planetary movement rather than their core personality.

They want to be around people, and they don't feel bad for saying what needs to be said, but when they fly off the handle, which happens most often when mercury is in retrograde or in their house, they know they need to fix things with certain characters.

As a friend of a Sagittarius, someone might experience one of these situations:

> • Flawless friends with the occasional disagreement of opinions

- Unbroken friendship with a few big fights a year when the planets are causing trouble.

- Solid friendship with no quarrels, but you know you're not their "best" friend.

- Close friendship that often feels as though they're at risk of losing friends who will eventually clutch too tight and drive the Sagittarius away.

The pattern is that the Sagittarius will often fix their conflicts or overcome disagreements with their closest friends only. Suppose one of their acquaintances has a disagreement. There, the Sagittarius will usually not see it as an investment to recover the friendship if the other person doesn't want to work for it. Essentially, they know what they bring to the table and how great of a friend they are, so they expect people to put in the effort too.

On another level, Sagittarians have a great sense of humor, and they're always good for a laugh. Famous comedian and Sagittarian Richard Pryor is absolute proof, but other comedians include Tiffany Haddish, Patrice O'Neal, and Ron White. They get people to laugh without trying, and they often prompt other individuals to explore their talents with humor too. They often have that perfect sense of timing for joking around, even though they don't understand that when it happens to regular conversation, but they approach all things in life with the thought of fun and comedy.

A lot of their comedy is for their friends. Sagittarians want to make their companions laugh, and they want to see people have a good time around them. They'll be outlandish and say the things that everyone is thinking but doesn't want to say. It's that approach to comedy and humor that makes so many people want to be buddies with a Sagittarius.

Sometimes, a Sagittarius friend might seem a little overwhelming or overbearing. Sagittarians want to fix everything, and sometimes they'll crack jokes in inappropriate situations when it is clearly not the moment. They do that because, in their mind, it's a way to work out the situation, to make it less sad or less frustrating. Sagittarius natives also don't understand that they need not fix every problem for their allies.

Often, a person may only need the Sagittarius to listen. They could take a note here and spend more time listening in to their friends rather than jumping straight into the action. Meanwhile, their companions might be a little more direct when they don't need help but just a listening ear.

Sagittarius Friendship Compatibility

Like all other signs, when it comes to compatibility, they're widely compatible and get along with many more individuals than other signs. Here is a complete guide to a Sagittarius' relationships with other types.

Aries

Fire signs burn bright together, and although they may not be lifelong friends, they can have a great time partying. These two will match each other in terms of energy and a love for fun. A Sagittarius and Aries will connect when adventuring and going through everything with little planning and zero care for what else is happening in the world.

They are excellent friends but may go long periods of time without seeing each other. The only trouble is that the Aries may not enjoy the eclipse of power that happens with these two.

Taurus

Taurus and Sagittarius are usually not a good mix. Scorched earth is the best way to describe what happens when this earth sign and fire sign get together. The Taurus thrives in familiarity and material possessions. Whereas the Sagittarius sees material items as a chain to any particular space, it's an anchor, and they hate that. And the

Taurus is exceptionally stubborn, and that gets under the Sagittarian's skin. Overall, very low compatibility.

Gemini

The Gemini sign is astrologically opposite from Sagittarius, and in a true opposites-attract moment, they do rather well together. A Gemini will complement the Sagittarian traits. You both seek what the others has. The Gemini wants the Sagittarian openness and humor, while the Sagittarian wants the Gemini's skill mastery and focus.

Cancer

Cancers are the whirlwind of emotions and compassion, which is everything the Sagittarius isn't. Sagittarians aren't slow-moving. They have little connection to the moon and can't stand sensitive people. That is everything that a Cancerian embodies. There is hope for this combination. Cancer might be that lone best friend that a Sagittarian has for their emotional needs and because Sagittarians can often help this sign.

Both signs love food, and they prefer the serenity of the outdoors. When these two get together, they can talk about the deep things in life, such as human nature, religion, and concepts that go beyond the physical plane.

If you have a Cancer friend, know that a Cancerian needs space the same way you do. Being too needy will often result in trouble as a Cancer wants time alone the same way that you want freedom.

Leo

To describe this powerhouse couple, we need only look at a few of the most infamous fictional or real-life couples. Think of Thelma and Louis, or Bonnie and Clyde, and that would accurately depict these two together. They brim with energy, they want to party, they're outgoing, and they're fierce friends. They could be best friends if the Leo of the group can stop themselves from becoming possessive. Leos want their friends around all the time, and for a Sagittarius, that might be too much quality time.

Virgo

A Virgo is a cautious planner, they want to know exactly what is going, and a Sagittarius just can't deliver that. But a Virgo is one of the very few who can appreciate the unfiltered opinion and insight that a Sagittarius provides. They are equally honest and forthcoming and understand that it's honesty, not abrasiveness.

Libra

Libras are dependable and aren't quick to jump to conclusions. There's a mutual agreement in this friendship that you can be good friends for a long time through honesty. Is this your best friend? Not really. Libras are notoriously low energy. They don't want to go on crazy adventures, or go out partying all the time. And there could be trouble with the Libras tendency to embarrassment.

Scorpio

Where Sagittarians always see the good in life and the possibilities of what could come, Scorpios are the opposite. You're Piglet, and they're Eeyore. So, can you two get along with each other? In many ways, yes. You are both prone to fighting, but you also both enjoy proving the other person wrong, so it could be a shared passion. The act of irritating others and each other could cause monstrous fights where one will eventually come around, and then they can start all over.

Sagittarius

Even better together! Sagittarius pairs will continuously push each other to do better, go bigger, and adventure more. Two Sagittarius natives together are unstoppable.

Capricorn

Capricorns find comfort in having their possessions nearby, and that stick to proven methods. Sagittarians love the novel and new, so they don't mix well with Capricorns, although they can rely on a Capricorn for useful insight on how to make the most of their strengths. Capricorns are good advisors to Sagittarians, although the Sagittarius native may not always want to hear what they have to say.

Aquarius

A fire sign and an air sign can make a fire tornado, and this mix is a great match. As friends, they're often adventurous together, and the Aquarius will usually present the planning and management that Sagittarians lack. They can put together travel plans and make sure they both have the right documents and budgeting to enjoy their trip. These two will push each other to explore, and the Sagittarian will help the Aquarian forget others' judgments.

Pisces

A true water sign that likes to put a flame out, Pisces can't take Sagittarian-level honesty, and they want nothing to do with crazy adventures. They party and they do have deep spiritual ties, which is where these two can connect. It's likely that this will be a passing harmony rather than a lifelong affair.

When Friends Fight

Sagittarians make good friends, even the best of partners, and it's common that they'll have many people happy to jump into friendship quickly, but there's always the chance of a fight. Sagittarians love to prove people wrong, and it's not even that they like being "right". They love the thrill of aiming to show someone exactly how they're wrong. They do fight often, and sometimes it's because they've taken a joke too far.

Being a Friend as a Sagittarius

- Understand that others aren't as open with communication – both receiving and giving

- Know that you need a diverse collection of friends to ensure that you're not alienating a few or overwhelming others.

Being a Friend to a Sagittarius

• Take the blunt honesty as an act of love, they love you and want you to succeed or thrive, and they think they're helping.

• Take a break when you can't keep up. It will only cause problems.

• Absorb the little things that Sagittarians do, like their generosity or optimism.

But when a Sagittarius fights with someone they care for, they are quick to make up and resolve the issue. Fire signs work with optimism and are often the ones who will work to make something right, even if they don't necessarily think they were wrong. A fire sign can acknowledge they were too aggressive or pushed too far. To them, a great friend is always worth a bit of humbleness or an apology.

On a final note, don't take their jokes too seriously, and give them space to support their freedom. You will lose a Sagittarius as a friend in two ways. You could be too clingy or dependent, or you could be too sensitive. If you find their jokes offensive, then it might not be a good match because the Sagittarius will not be pushed into stopping what comes so naturally to them. Sagittarians will always be their true self, so they won't do much to adapt to their friends' needs.

Chapter 8: Sagittarius in Love

A Sagittarius is notorious in love, perhaps for all the wrong reasons. It is not what it appears on the surface. Let's take a quick glance at what a relationship with a Sagittarius looks like from the outside and to the other person involved in the relationship.

The beginning of the affair is a whirlwind. The other person may not have even realized how fast and how hard they've fallen in love, or at least fallen into enthusiasm. Sagittarian's energy can suck in just about anyone, and they make people feel special. Who doesn't love that? Then, things slow down because the other individual needs a rest, and it seems like this is the settling of the water. It looks like you're done with the rapids and into the smooth and steady side of the river. And then it happens, they grow distant, and they break up with the person. What happened? From the outside, no one knows. It sounds like Sagittarius natives are just bad at romantic relationships because they're great friends, so just their lovers suffer this terrible fate.

From the inside of that relationship, it's a drastically different experience. If more people spent time looking at the Sagittarius in love rather than the lucky soul they've fallen in love with, they would see in an aggressive, fun, and confident person at the beginning of a relationship but once that honeymoon phase tapers off and the challenge is gone, the Sagittarius starts to see all the other qualities of their partner. They started to see that maybe they don't bring out the best in this other, and maybe this person isn't outgoing and extroverted but is instead a little reserved. That is when the Sagittarius distances themselves, and eventually, they leave.

When a Sagittarius is in a relationship or is flirting with someone and getting ready to enter a love union, they make their zest for life contagious. It's almost impossible to avoid the feeling of loving life and adventure when a Sagittarius falls for you. Sagittarians also enjoy spoiling their partners, and they do so with big gestures and a lot of generosity. Like most fire signs, Sagittarians love passion, but they won't stay in a relationship where either person must compromise any part of themselves.

It's that unwillingness to negotiate that makes Sagittarians seem so flighty. They are the ones holding out for that absolute perfect match, and they're fine waiting well into their later years to find it. If a partner starts pressuring them to enter an affair or to take their relationship to the next level, it's almost always the end of that part of their life.

Sagittarius Compatibility in Romance

Unsurprisingly, Sagittarians are highly compatible with many signs for short periods of time. But they link up with key signs for long moments of time, and that is what a Sagittarius should look for in a partner.

Aries

These relationships are fire, and these two will have a lot of fun spending weeks or months playing hard to get for each other. Neither takes anything personally, and they both need a lot of independence. Aries and Sagittarius are fairly compatible if Aries can control their jealousy, and Sagittarius doesn't ask too much of their partner.

Taurus

These two are great hookup buddies, but nothing beyond that. Venus and Jupiter align happily on sexual terms, but outside of that, this earth sign spells disaster for Sagittarius. While Taurus is often concerned with what other people think, Sagittarians don't care. These two will be nitpicking at each other quickly in a relationship.

Gemini

A relationship between a Sagittarius and Gemini is all about the mental connection. These two signs both have deep roots in spiritual affiliation and higher thinking, and that is where they find joy together. This is one of the few relationships where a Sagittarius native might spend more time conversing with their partner rather than having fun with a group of people.

Cancer

The trouble between Cancer and Sagittarius is that the Cancer would have to let go of a lot when it comes to emotional needs and expectations. A Sagittarius would not ask that of their partner, and so these two rarely work out very well. Basically, Cancerians look for supportive and nurturing environments, and they create routines that establish security. These drive a Sagittarius native out of their mind.

Leo

These two fire signs really can help each other utilize all their strengths and overcome common challenges for both signs. They are both outgoing, they both love to entertain and host parties, and they both enjoy doing new things. Of course, Leos tend to have a lazy side, but their need for alone time often means that they don't mind when the Sagittarius goes out and has fun without them.

For Sagittarians, Leo is the almost perfect match. If you find you may enjoy a long term relationship where neither of you has exceptionally high expectations of the other, and neither of you wants the other person to change. It's everything that a Sagittarius look for in a relationship.

Virgo

Virgos can match the quick wit of a Sagittarius, and they have a bit of humor so they can play off and enjoy banter together. The difference is that Virgos are more objective and analytical, and they might not give in to all of Sagittarians big thinking or breaking apart deep concepts. Otherwise, great conversations can quickly turn into a full out fight because the Virgo is asking "where's the proof" and the Sagittarius is playing the "what if" game.

Many people discount Sagittarius and Virgo's ability to click on a long-term level, specifically because many people observe that Virgos are reserved and tend to be quiet. The trouble is that usually they are composed and quiet in new situations, and once they

Libra

There are a few key issues with relationships between Libras and Sagittarians. First is the trouble of appearance. Sagittarians don't pay attention to what other individuals think about them, and they will often do whatever they please. Libra's care very much about what other individuals think of them and worry about their appearance, and how to handle themselves in public situations. They might be easily embarrassed by their Sagittarians partner, no matter how much they love them and enjoy their company.

The second issue is money. Dating a Libra can quickly become expensive, and Sagittarians don't have that much of a connection with material possessions. They may see the libra's shopping habits and spending habits as frivolous and that they are missing out on the finer things in life experienced because of material goods.

Scorpio

There is a deep sexual connection, but the novelty wears away over the first few months. This is a classic situation for Sagittarians. Scorpios are mysterious and stimulating and want to have deep conversations, but they don't have the energy or the outgoing nature that Sagittarians do. The Scorpio gets sucked into the Sagittarius vortex of vitality and optimism, and then eventually, the Sagittarius sees that the Scorpio is essentially the opposite of them. They don't want the Scorpio to compromise, and they are not willing to bargain, so the relationship ends.

Sagittarius

A Sagittarius dating a Sagittarius could be the start of a good joke. You're both a little flighty, neither one of you is great at commitment, neither one of you cared very much for money, and neither of you is very practical. It sounds like a recipe for disaster, but an underlying element could change the states for Sagittarius and Sagittarius relationship: moon signs.

Sagittarians don't deeply connect with their moon signs as they are not highly emotional people, but relationships are always emotion-driven, and when a Sagittarius and Sagittarius get together, their moon signs become more prominent in determining compatibility.

Capricorn

Capricorns and Sagittarius are the perfect setups of how opposites attract. Capricorns are careful, they plan, they analyze, and they look closely at risk. Sagittarians run headlong toward risk, and they don't care about analyzing or planning or being careful. But these two sides are deeply rooted in learning and experiencing new vantage points through the human experience. They love to learn from each other, and they love to see how the other one is often immovable in what they need from the relationship.

This is perhaps the highest compatibility that a Sagittarius could have except for Leo, and it's because Capricorns are dependable, ambitious, and committed. They return the loyalty, accountability, and honesty that Sagittarians provide. One famous Sagittarius-Capricorn couple is Chrissy Teigen and John Legend.

Aquarius

Aquarius is just as intense as you are, they are just as independent and adventurous, but they're passionate about different things. Most Aquarians are deeply rooted in family, and they aren't willing to budge in terms of managing their life around what they want to carry out. A relationship between an Aquarius and a Sagittarius could often result in a "ships passing in the night" situation.

Pisces

Philosophical, which can lead to interesting conversations, but these two don't click because Sagittarians are extremely self-confident, and Pisces are the opposite. They need reassurance, comfort, and support. A Sagittarian will not provide that for long.

Don't Misinterpret Commitment Signals

Sagittarians love to rush into things, but they are slow to commit. They're sometimes famously slow by being lifelong bachelors or bachelorettes. They're holding out for the best option. They are the kid at the candy store that could have any piece of candy, but they want that one that is going to hit the spot and leave them satisfied for a long time.

They also need someone who will fit in with their friend group and who won't feel alienated by being around friends often. Many signs associate romantic partnerships with privacy, but the partnership should just be an ever-present factor of their life to a Sagittarius. If they go out with friends, then their partners more than welcome to come. If their romantic partner doesn't want to spend time around their friends, then there is a problem because they're never going to see them.

Slightly Insecure and Needy

There is trouble that comes up in a romantic relationship that doesn't appear in any other element of a Sagittarius life. Insecurity. Sagittarians are always confident, and they have no problem jumping into unknown situations with bravado. But, after a couple of failed partnerships, it's common that Sagittarians get a little insecure.

After a few failed relationships, it's likely that the Sagittarius will begin to panic as soon as they feel that the honeymoon phase is ending. They'll dwell on whether they invested too much of themselves and the possibility that the other person got bored with them.

They'll wonder if they should end the relationship now to save on heartache later. Why aren't they calling, texting, or doing exciting things the way they used to? These are the questions that will invade a Sagittarian's mind when they see the honeymoon is done, and time to build a life together.

The only cure for this is to understand that your past relationships didn't work out because you were resistant to compromise, and you were unwilling to let someone else compromise for you. That is a very noble reason to let relationships go, and it's better to have let them slip by if it means finding that one great love of your life later.

If you feel like you're becoming too needy because of this insecurity, communicate it with your partner. Explain that you don't know where the relationship is going, but that you feel the need to spend more time around them, and you want to keep that honeymoon phase going. The honeymoon phase can't last forever, but you certainly can work with your partner to keep things new and interesting.

What Sagittarians Need in a Relationship

More than anything else, a Sagittarian needs a commitment rooted in trust. They cannot have someone frequently asking them where they're going and what they're doing. They will not put up with that for long and will bail on the relationship quickly; that said, Sagittarians aren't necessarily one for open relationships. They want to live independently alongside one other person. They need to bring out the best in that other person while also being the best version of themselves, and it's difficult to find that with one person, so why would they try it with multiple people?

A Sagittarius native will also require clear and blunt communication throughout the entirety of their relationship. This will help aid the level of independence they need, as both parties will understand exactly what the other needs. Finally, when it comes to communicating love, Sagittarians crave physical comfort and small reminders. They don't need grand gestures, and they rarely look for the other individual to go out of their way. They want the kiss at the door before someone leaves the house and the nice text message halfway through the day just to know that the other person was thinking of them.

Chapter 9: Sagittarius, the Life of the Party

Sagittarians know that high-energy activities, spontaneity, and a zeal for life come naturally to them. From the outside, other signs might see Sagittarius natives as simple party animals. Their high intensity and their overzealous personalities make them the spotlight of most parties and well-known in many party circles. These are the people who will know where the celebration is and who is going to be there. The level of electricity is hard for anyone else to match except for in the party scene. At these events Sagittarius natives find their equals in terms of intensity and presence.

Sagittarius born is the OG party animal, the ones who want to jump onto a table, riding the mechanical bull, start the dancing at a big party, or dare the rest into getting into the party mood. Overall, other signs have little chance of slowing down a Sagittarius. They're simply too much of a force. They're unstoppable, much like the Archer. If they want to achieve something, they will certainly do it.

Those born to the Sagittarius sign know that partying brings out the essence of their soul, and they need everyone else to operate on their level. Sagittarians are often the first to suggest a party or gathering, even a calm one. They want everyone together, and to vibe off the collection of high-energy and good moods that come together at a celebration.

Sagittarians Thrive in the "Party" Scene

Those under the Sagittarius sign don't just love parties. It's where they thrive. If you could work through your early years hosting or planning events or slinging drinks at a bar, those might be a few of your fondest memories.

What should other signs expect from Sagittarius party scenes? Think underground New York or West Hollywood. Now, Sagittarians don't need to "fit" the scene to make an appearance. If they hear there's a party, then they're heading out. For example, they may often head out to a rave without even liking Electric Dance Music.

Besides thriving in the party scene, they have an odd approach to the scene's seedy underside. Sagittarius are natural thrill-seekers and gamblers, but they aren't exceptionally prone to habit-forming addictions because they don't like feeling dependent on anything. Although a Sagittarius might repeatedly try or experiment with drugs or drink to excess, they will often identify when they must reel in that behavior.

It may be difficult for Sagittarius natives to understand that more is not always more. They are prone to get hooked into a variety of behaviors, so it's important to be aware of that challenge.

Alternatively, if they have fallen into addiction, their loyalty to those closest to them will often spur them to correct the behavior before too long. Sagittarians and their friends or family should keep an eye out for the early signs of addiction or dangerous activity with experimenting in the party scene.

Always the Ones to Go Out but Don't Expect a Routine

Without a doubt, Sagittarius is the wild child in the group in the zodiac. They hit the party scene regularly, but not in any routine way. Sagittarius' hate routine in every element of their life and that happens with partying too. They won't hit the same clubs on the same nights, and they won't make a habit of doing the same things repeatedly. Instead, they prefer all their free-time unscheduled so they can do what they want.

This works out exceptionally well for their friends because it means they can always count on a good time, but never know what's in store. Sagittarians are also laid back, so if someone else does want to do something specific, they can usually go with the flow and accept the unexpected plans.

Routines are among Sagittarius' top dislikes. They hate routine and will avoid it at all costs. About going to parties: it means that they're the ones who shake things up and bring people out of their routines to make sure that everyone, including themselves, has a good time.

Sagittarians also dislike people who think they need to please others, so any "plastic people" present in the group will quickly be called out or dismissed. They make it easy for everyone to enjoy themselves as long as they're not judging anyone else.

Sagittarians Bring the Party

Sagittarians make parties and "make" parties. They don't have a problem for handling, organizing, and hosting a party. Sagittarians often enjoy planning and hosting. They are among the best hosts in the zodiac with close contenders of Pisces and Leo, but they can make another's event a hit. They are explorers of new experiences and can often think up new games or conversation starters on the spot. If they walk into a party that was just getting started or that hasn't yet gained momentum, then it will certainly reach its full swing shortly after a Sagittarius shows up!

They're the ones who encourage other people to try new things too. Sagittarius natives will get people on the dance floor, having deep and engaging conversations, and interacted in party games that are fun.

Be Wary of Philosophical and Political Conversation

Sagittarius natives are exceptionally prone to getting into deep conversations. Unfortunately, they're not the savvy conversationalist for these kinds of topics. They have strong opinions and rarely take much consideration into other's opinions. Political conversations rarely go well for Sagittarians, which is unfortunate because even though they don't listen well during these exchanges, they are genuinely interested in learning.

With this matter, Sagittarians may not realize that they're bringing the conversation down or becoming aggressive. That is, until they're in a full-blown argument where they've lost complete control of themselves and killed the party vibe. They are a huge risk when around others with strong political or philosophical views. Now, when not at a party, these people can get along great and dive deeply into conversations that make a lot of other people uncomfortable, but these topics aren't for all types of events. Many people just want to have a good time and get a break from deep or political conversations. But their blunt and abrasive way of carrying conversations usually means these conversations will kill the mood.

How to Help a Sagittarius with a Party

Because Sagittarians are so good at celebrations, it is a common occurrence that they'll plan something, or someone will ask them to plan their event. Many signs that see their prowess for this will want to jump in and support, but how can you help without diminishing the Sagittarian charm that makes this party so great?

The best way to help a Sagittarius with a party is to ask directly. Say, "What can I do to help with the party planning?" As Sagittarius is so direct with their communication, you can be sure to get a direct answer. You must communicate as directly as the Sagittarius, from food to the invite list. They might want updates or check-in to see if you need help. That's not because they don't trust you; it's because they have so much energy they probably planned to do everything themselves and are surprised that things are moving so quickly.

Another way to help is to show your support. Never has there been a fire sign that didn't soak up the occasional compliment. Sagittarians don't care what others think, but they do acknowledge it when other people appreciate them.

A genuine compliment can help the Sagittarius buck up on any sore feelings that might have happened in the planning process. Many elements of party planning are sure to go wrong. For example, if they were planning a gathering and told everyone it was a potluck, then it's sure that someone won't bring something, or two people will bring highly competing dishes. The Sagittarian, in this example, might feel as though it's not so difficult to follow directions. They might feel that their guests should be able to follow the simple directions of bringing a dish, or even get a little heated about it. A compliment from a friend can heal that wound and bring down the desire to lash out. When they feel wronged, they'll stop at nothing to take action or get revenge against them. But as a close friend, you have the power to bring them down, to get them back into the partying mood, and move on from the hurt feelings.

When Should Sagittarians Avoid a Party?

Sometimes, a Sagittarius should just avoid the party altogether, but when is that? A Virgo, Aquarius, and a Taurus throw a party, and the Sagittarius stayed home. They should consider who will be at the celebration before they go. If they know that someone will be there who they can't stand, they should sit this one out. They shouldn't try to force a good time, and the middle of a party is not the time to make amends or sort out why you two don't get along.

Sagittarians should also avoid parties that primarily have introverts or homebodies. If these people don't like going out and actively avoid it, then you won't have much fun. That party will shut down early, and you might be left with a night that has no plans, and it's too late to go on an adventure.

Sagittarians need not be at every celebration, even though they want to be. If they have addiction issues, they may need to separate themselves from the scene, and find another outlet to be around people in good spirits without a lot of opportunity for substance or alcohol presence.

The thing is that Sagittarius natives don't need substances or alcohol to have a good time. They do it for themselves, but they can fall into these habits, and it can be a hard struggle to face.

Key Sagittarius Partying Take-Aways

Overall, the Sagittarians party often and party hard. They turn it up to eleven, they dance all night, and their energy really gives a positive surge to everyone around them but they should watch out for the possibility of getting too attached to the party lifestyle because it can put a damper on other life areas.

There is also the risk these abrasive and blunt individuals will turn conversations sour at a party. It happens occasionally, and usually, there's no saving the event after that. They simply will feel like they stuck their foot in their mouth, and then they might feel bad throughout the rest of the party. And they could get the urge to prove that other attendees wrong and just blatantly attack the other person with their intellect and opinions, which is unfair in the best of times. Other signs simply aren't prepared for that battle, but a Sagittarius is always ready to dominate a conversation on politics or philosophy.

Sagittarians should go out often for their mental health. They need to be around many people in good spirits where they can expel their energy. As they do this, they'll feel more in line with the rawest version of themselves. Sagittarius natives will do best when they're surrounded by many friends.

Chapter 10: Sagittarian Career Paths

The Centaur has countless career paths that could suit them well, but which is really the right one? You need the opportunity to think freely, constantly improve, and seek out rewarding changes. But what career can deliver that? Where can you travel, have adventures, and explore the need to learn and dive into the higher mind elements?

Your sign is that of the traveler who aims for big goals and often succeeds. Sitting still is possibly your biggest challenge in the workplace. Many Sagittarians find comfort in being an entrepreneur and may even open businesses with the express plan of selling them for a profit within a few years so as not to get tied down. As a visionary, you're often the one who comes up with solutions to problems that seem like a dead end and the ideas for new products or services that truly meet the customers' needs.

Sagittarius has a distinctive association with career and money. In general, they don't have much of a mind for it—usually, they are drawn to careers involving long-term plans and cooperating with other people. Sagittarians make excellent friends, but whether they make great coworkers or employees is yet to be seen.

Sagittarius with Career and Money

Sagittarius natives have key factors within their core personality that directly impact their career paths and their relationship with money. The most significant factor is their inability to concentrate on one single interest. Again, these factors circle back to Jupiter, the ruling planet, and the ties to learning as much as they can. Many Sagittarians feel as though they have a very limited measure of time to learn all the universe's secrets. Because of that feeling, they'll pick up hobbies left and right, and their interests will build up quickly. It's important that a Sagittarius learn to focus on two or three primary interests that can tie in with many smaller hobbies. For example, most Sagittarius' love to travel, and they can do this through a career that involves frequent travel. They can enjoy local food and getting to know the local customs during their travels.

One book that directly addresses a lot of what Sagittarians need in a career is called <u>Doing Work You Love</u>. It calls for that inner passion for coming out and focuses on how Sagittarians feel the need to flee from job to job because they are not satisfied.

As the sign which represents higher education and the stronger mind, it's likely that a Sagittarius will feel more rewarded and more complete in a position where they can learn. Working as a teacher, religious official, or in a cutting edge industry such as gaming or technology will allow you to learn new things all the time. It may even demand it. There is the ongoing belief that Sagittarians thrive in publishing, but the industry has changed dramatically over the last 100 years. Now publishing often involves sitting at a desk for many hours a day and making phone calls. It is not the over- the-top getting the paper out on time environment that it once was.

But Sagittarians are known as wordsmiths, and famous Sagittarian wordsmiths include Mark Twain, Jay-Z, Taylor Swift, and Winston Churchill. With public speaking, Sagittarians truly *thrive*, and they often are happy to set out on performance because, in truth, they're just themselves.

With specific projects, Sagittarius natives excel with projects with many small goals. Sagittarians would be well suited as a project manager with various construction companies or companies that are expanding quickly. Your follow-through skills may not be ideal for project management opportunities, but your ability to work closely with people and to negotiate compromise makes your talent to perform exceptional.

Sagittarius natives reap the benefits of Jupiter's good luck with money. They care little for money, and they aren't extraordinarily interested in physical products or possessions. They usually buy what they need – and occasionally buy something they like. Like other fire signs, they have a very generous nature and likely enjoy shopping for others more than for themselves. That relationship with money plays into their career path because many Sagittarians aren't connected to their job or career on a monetary basis. They may leave one job for a job that pays less but offers more intrinsic rewards such as exploring new topics or leading a team.

Perhaps it is because they care so little about money is that they consistently seem to have it. Sagittarians would much rather spend cash on adventures such as camping, traveling, going out with friends, and once in a lifetime experiences like bungee jumping. Sagittarius natives always seem to have enough money to do what they want and be generous, but if it's the choice between changing jobs and not being able to travel as often, it's a clear choice. For the situation of staying with a job where they don't have as much freedom as they would like and having money, they would leave the job and have less capital rather than reduced freedom.

Who is the Sagittarius in the Workplace?

As an employee, the Sagittarius is the wild card. These will put together the absolute best holiday parties and remember things like Administrative Appreciation Day or Food Service Appreciation Week. It's likely that it's a Sagittarius in charge of putting together who decorates a desk or car for a birthday or an anniversary. Sagittarians love to celebrate and make people around them excited to be doing what they're doing. Having a Sagittarius as a coworker is absolutely amazing unless they are ready to leave.

When Sagittarius is disgruntled, they are usually biding their time, and it might be because of how loyal they are to their coworkers. Sagittarians are loyal almost to a fault, and they may spend time in a position they don't like or under a manager they can't stand because they feel like they are serving as a buffer for the rest of their coworkers. If they see that a boss is around pushing their coworker, they'll be the first ones to stand up and defend them. Additionally, if they know that a good manager isn't getting the respect or appreciation they deserve, they will be the first one to say something to the team.

For managers, this bluntness and unpredictability cause quite a bit of trouble. Sagittarians aren't motivated by money, so supervisors usually know they can't buy these people off with a raise. Additionally, there might be motivation towards accepting a promotion, but you can never tell with a Sagittarius. If they are happy with their position and think a promotion would restrict their freedom, then they'll take a pass and won't accept it.

Managers are often left wondering exactly what's continuing to happen when they go into a meeting because they don't know how that Sagittarian will react. But the Sagittarius native will have a lot to say, and they will not hold back. The best way to manage a Sagittarius is to provide intrinsic rewards. Let them hold a party, have more freedom, have a little more time at the water cooler. They are likely providing you with superior work, so it is well deserved that they get a little extra here in there.

Particular Challenges That Can Direct Career Paths

We have come back to the particular demands that plague Sagittarius natives throughout their lives. First, they are restless. Second, they need to excel and move forward, but they don't wish to be tied to any one company or entity, and finally, they are impatient. What are the Sagittarius to do?

Initially, they should prioritize what they value most in their personality and what type of jobs they could find to benefit that personality aspect.

Here's an example that lists many of the most common values that Sagittarius natives look for in a job or career:

- Ability to work outdoors
- Travel frequently
- Freedom to change schedules as needed
- Ability to help people
- Ability to learn new things
- Variety in daily work
- Big goals

When Sagittarians can list the things they are looking for in a career, they can focus on what's most important to them and eliminate the noise. For example, the person may be interested in landscaping work, working as a Park Ranger, providing tours of a local attraction or natural feature, or even doing work with the local government such as waterworks.

Now, if the list above looked more like:

- Helping people
- Learning
- Traveling
- Working outdoors
- Big goals

A list like this one might guide a Sagittarian into teaching, specifically teaching abroad. Many Sagittarius natives do religious work, which constantly delivers a lot of traveling opportunities, the chances to help communities, and a lifelong learning experience.

The core element here is to take what is most important and then assess the different career paths that are most closely aligned with your sun sign.

Hating Routines and Overly Organized Elements of Life

Usually, the driving factor of whether a Sagittarian can make a job a career is how much routine is in place. If the job involves the same morning routine, that might be fine. But the same routine throughout the whole day will quickly drive away a Sagittarius, even if they love the job. They hate the overly organized environment and simply can't stand working for "Type-A" people.

The trouble with this is that the Sagittarius native will feel confined within their job, and that's the majority of where adults spend their time. If they can't have freedom in their workplace, then they might feel as though their entire life is planned out, and they've reached the end of their freedom streak before they've hit thirty. Sagittarians have a knack for exploding situations way out of proportion.

Make Your Own Way

One exceptionally famous Sagittarian has shown the tried and tested method that would work for nearly any Sagittarius... Walt Disney. He not only made a name for himself, but engaged in public speaking often. He was creative, had complete freedom in his work schedule, and controlled every aspect of his business. He worked with people he chose and found joy in connecting with others through storytelling. Walt Disney embodied nearly every career element that a Sagittarius could want. It's well-known that once Disneyland was established, he would often walk the grounds and spend time outside.

Another famous Sagittarian who forged that same path is Andrew Carnegie. He was not only one of America's most noteworthy industrialists who revolutionized the steel industry, but he was also one of the leading philanthropists of his time. He worked several jobs before finding his love for the steel industry. Those jobs included working as a telegraph operator and Railroad Superintendent.

Top Jobs for Sagittarius

These really spell out the basics of what a Sagittarius need in a job. A Sagittarian may thrive in any of these positions, but your personal interests and passions should direct you toward a career you can love for life.

Architects

Sagittarians are exceptionally creative souls with problem-solving. Architects often work far beyond the building's standard structure and often work alongside those implementing the "nuts and bolts" of the building. They're looking for ways to make these buildings visually appealing while also unbelievably useful. They fit into design-based roles, but they have trouble because design jobs often mean small amounts of travel, and it means sitting behind a desk. Those are two things that Sagittarian's hate.

On the other hand, an architect will also be on the scene during construction and oversee many project elements. Similar to a project manager, this gives the architect a leadership-type position while also allowing them to be on a construction-site at irregular intervals.

Then there's the final element that the architecture and building industry design is constantly changing. The design elements that are trendy or popular are constantly changing, and that's something that Sagittarians truly enjoy.

Grade School Teacher

As a grade-school teacher, you could control each day and make sure that your routines embrace your need for freedom, and you get to share that with the children. Having the ability to get creative and bring excitement into a classroom can fit in with many Sagittarians. Additionally, teachers usually have a lot of freedom for taking their classes outside for science and art projects.

As a teacher, you could explore your passion for learning every day and help kids build that excitement as well.

Theology Based Careers

Those born under Jupiter connect deeply with theology, and you might feel inclined to explore religious or theological careers. Working within a church or within the studies of religion can, surprisingly, come with a lot of travel. Additionally, you can affect the lives of countless people, even if you're only looking to validate information or spread the word.

This career path is common among Sagittarians, as it allows them to immerse themselves in communities. They don't even have to work in association with a church, but through theological research, a Sagittarius could easily connect with and help many people in need.

Sports Coach, Life Coach, or Personal Trainer

Sagittarians love helping people be their best "self", and you can carry out just that as a coach. As a life coach, sports coach, or personal trainer, you can connect directly with someone who needs a boost, and give them what they need. You can teach others how to build new skills and devote themselves to bettering their life. This career path can also keep you outside a lot and often comes with freedom with your schedule.

A Combination for Interests for a Career, Not Just a Job

Sagittarius loves humanitarian work or doing good for others, and they can find many jobs where this is an ever-present element, but that doesn't mean that you'll be happy with the first non-profit job that comes along. Instead, look for a job that allows you to do good while still exploring the many elements of life that interest you. Just because you're a Sagittarian doesn't mean that you must sign up for missionary work. If you're not very religious, then it's not likely a good fit. But you can find several organizations that allow you to travel and help others with good pay, and no travel expenses.

Ideally, you'll can have a lot of paths to follow. Sagittarius natives love the ability to keep their options open. Don't over commit to one company. Instead, devote yourself to an industry or something you're passionate about rather than one enterprise, or one institution.

Chapter 11: The Great Zodiac Shift and Ophiuchus

Way back in the 1970s, people discussed a 13th sign. Then in about 2014, NASA stepped in and put their foot in it. The great Zodiac shift impacts Sagittarians more than almost any other sign in the zodiac because this 13th sign is present through most of the Sagittarius in range.

Are there 13 signs in the zodiac? There are many reasons the ancient civilizations responsible for astrology's foundation omitted the 13th sign. There is an overwhelming mathematical balance in having 12 signs rather than 13. With 12 signs, there are four primary elements, and each element has three signs. And there are three modalities, and each modality has four signs. Each sign is represented by a planetary body in our immediate solar system, as there are 12 heavenly bodies in the solar system if you include the sun and the moon. Ancient civilizations also used 12 signs for the zodiac as it accurately represented the 12-month calendar they used during that period of time. This is true among Babylonians, Egyptians, Greeks, and Romans.

So why is everyone still talking about this 13th sign? Each time the 13th sign, Ophiuchus, is brought up, it becomes about whether ancient civilizations knew about this sign. The answer is yes, Ophiuchus has historical roots, the constellation is historically acknowledged, and it has a presence in the universal set up for astrology.

In 2014, NASA underwent more scrutiny and publicity when it announced that the zodiac was done wrong. The statement was not made to undermine astrology, which NASA doesn't acknowledge as a science, anyway. The message was more of a fun historical fact segment, and they didn't mean to cause the stir that happened. They saw it as a fun insight into history, and many within the astrological community took it as a personal offense.

Part of the problem with the 2014 report is what happened in the 1970s. The idea was present it to the public as though it was new; as if these ancient civilizations were not aware of this 13th sign and had accidentally omitted it.

Ophiuchus has always been present in the heavens, and its position along the ecliptic was well-documented among ancient civilizations. It simply wasn't selected among early astrologers. Ironically, it is one of the classic arguments against astrology where astrology lists and non-believers can agree. This sign was not chosen with a purpose, and even 4,000 years ago, astrology and astronomy were different things. Today, astronomy is a very scientific and mathematically driven field. Although they are the foundations of science and mathematics in astrology, historical presence and information give us a different view of the same heavenly bodies. Astronomists classify planets and consider the various aspects of life and the environment. Astrologists look at how the universe affects *people* directly.

Many people have a ton of questions about Ophiuchus, and it's well worth exploring how exactly this constellation and its movement can affect a Sagittarius native.

Did NASA Really Change the Zodiac?

No, NASA came out and stated that they didn't change the zodiac. They were just making an observation. The space agency came out and announced that it wouldn't change astrology because it doesn't deal with astrology. Their business is astronomy, and they felt it was a thought-provoking and fun experience. All the same, they cultivate quite a lot of talk.

The zodiac and the universe are not accurately represented on a flat piece of paper. The ancients did the best they could with the tools and resources they had. For 4,000 years, each new generation refined and improved the zodiac's visual representation until about the 1600s, which delivered the modern model of the zodiac with the circle that shows the elements, modalities, the symbols of each sun sign.

What is Ophiuchus?

The sign Ophiuchus falls from November 29th to December 18th and three additional cusp dates on either side. Most Sagittarius natives are inadvertently affected by Ophiuchus in one way or another, even though the zodiac hasn't changed.

Ophiuchus is not like any other sign within the zodiac, mostly because it's not a sun sign. But, moving aside from that, the constellation illustrates an actual person that historians can prove to have existed. The sign also represents a humanoid figure, which aside from Aquarius, makes it the only other sign to do so.

Ophiuchus is directly associated with and represents Imhotep, the royal vizier. Imhotep was well-documented as an astrologer, architect, sage, and the second King within Egypt's third dynasty. After his death around 2600 BCE, he was worshipped as a god of medicine in Egypt and Greece. Ophiuchus was the illegitimate child of Apollo or a demi-God who would sail the seas bringing life through legend.

The sign Ophiuchus differs dramatically from other sun signs because it has no element and does not belong to a common modality. Additionally, it doesn't have an opposing sign. In Greece, it was known not directly as Ophiuchus but instead as Serpentarius, the Serpent Bearer.

The imbalance of this thirteenth sign breaks away from many of the structured elements of the zodiac.

Ophiuchus Personality Traits

Ophiuchus is the rare sign to depict an actual man; even Aquarius, as the water bearer, only represents the idea of a man. This has led many to become jealous of Ophiuchus because they are believed to possess Ophiuchus's wisdom, specifically with matters of medicine and science. If that sounds familiar, then you're on the right track as Sagittarians already have an innate curiosity, and much of that could be attributed to Ophiuchus.

Typically, one should expect an Ophiuchus native to have an insatiable knowledge for wisdom and learning. That lines up directly with Sagittarian traits. Other common elements among this sign are a good sense of humor, a touch of jealousy, and an openness to change, but they take on a few Scorpio traits, including an explosive temper and a high inclination toward an inflated ego.

Overall, they often show:

- Curiosity and a desire to obtain new wisdom
- Great family connections
- Good luck
- Visionary problem-solving skills
- Innate ability to interpret dreams.

Strange Elements of the Ophiuchus Sign

Ophiuchus is both passionate and smart, but there are plenty of odd traits about them, which mark them as different from all the rest. We've mentioned that they have no element, and they have no modality, although they seem to fit within the mutable modality along most accurately with Sagittarius.

Their element-less nature can make them seem like exceptionally bland people. Not just at first, many people report that Ophiuchus natives might just be less interesting than those who are purely Sagittarian. Taylor Swift falls square into the Ophiuchus dates, and many people wonder who she is behind the red lipstick. It's well-known that she's not responsible for all or most of her songs and has led a very secretive life off-stage. Even she reports that she's not very interesting.

In that same nod, you have Ozzy Osbourne, which is alarmingly interesting. Why are there drastically different results from the same factors? Many bring it down to their lack of element.

To give this context, water signs are notoriously emotional in both good and bad ways. Scorpio, Pisces, and Cancer are the water signs, and they are all either internally emotionally high strung or an external ball of emotion. Air signs, including Gemini, Libra, and Aquarius, spend most of their time thinking. They're logical and communicate well, but their intelligence leads them into complicated conundrums often. Fire signs, including Aries, Leo, and Sagittarius, are passionate, loyal, and a bit fiery. Whereas earth signs, including Taurus, Virgo, and Capricorn, are rooted in the physical world, things they can see, and accomplishments they can prove. They're often extremely productive and work-oriented.

Given the nature of those born to the Ophiuchus sign, many people assume that they belong to the fire collection. They tend to be passionate, but not in any static way. You can't say that Ophiuchus is passionate about family and luxury how Leos are, or passionate about fairness how Aries are, or they share the same passion for independence and freedom how Sagittarians do.

Could This Explain Sagittarius' Eccentric and Unpredictable Nature?

Absolutely. Not having an element means that there's nothing grounding them together, but it certainly explains how Sagittarians can have such a drastically wider scale when it comes to personalities than other signs. Other signs were affected by the zodiac shift, but remember, there wasn't much of an actual shift. In fact, many of those who are Pisces now would have been Pisces back in the 1600s – or even the 800s.

The difference with Sagittarius and the other sun signs is that Sagittarius, for the most part, involves Ophiuchus. Ophiuchus naturally falls within the date range that ancients laid out for the sun signs.

What to do if You're a Sagittarius-Ophiuchus?

If you find that you're a Sagittarius also born within the Ophiuchus dates, there are things you can do to curb the negative elements of this under-examined sign. First, put jealousy aside because it's the trait most associated with Ophiuchus that isn't already in your wheelhouse. Second, carefully consider your interests. If you've spent a life dedicated to science and medicine, then you might have more in tune with this planet-less and element-less sign than your fellow Sagittarians.

Finally, you might dedicate a particular time to exploring this sign on your own. Remember that it's possible to interact with Ophiuchus in your moon sign and your ascending sign. Overall, we know that Ophiuchus natives spend a lot of time independently and alone. They appreciate their privacy and show very focused interests rather than the Sagittarius sign's fleeting interests. There are many opportunities for those of the Ophiuchus sign, as they are often extremely concentrated and accomplish goals easily.

Chapter 12: Thriving Sagittarians

Sagittarians represent the growth of the human spirit and the development of belief. They cultivate liberation and optimism wherever they go. They're the sunflowers that turn their face to the sun, and they help everyone around them do the same. A Sagittarius will refuse to sell themselves short or meet social norms if it doesn't naturally fit in with who they are. They see the bigger picture and value themselves, but they understand and can align it with everyday situations and people.

A Sagittarius will use their philosophical mind to help solve problems in social situations. They'll also turn to their good humor to that relieve tension in many cases. Sometimes this can go too far and get them in a bit of trouble, but Jupiter's gift of luck and the fire element's gift of charisma helps them out of many sticky situations.

Overall, they wish to encourage others to see the good in things and strive to live their best lives. That's all they want to see in life is everyone exploring their highest selves. They want no one to wear a mask in public or change their behavior based on another person's opinion, and they would love for everyone to chase their dreams and go on wild adventures. They do have trouble when it comes to encouraging others to do things they think they should do. Even with this minor setback, Sagittarians make good friends because of their optimistic and inspiring nature.

Sagittarians rarely have any problem thriving wherever they are until they feel trapped. They may feel caged in and a need to run. It's the horse aspect of their centaur symbol. They need wide open spaces, lots of freedom, and little rules or restrictions in life.

Time to Play and Lots of Freedom

The first thing that a Sagittarius needs to thrive is the opportunity to play a lot. They want to have fun, and that usually happens in social settings. A Sagittarius native may have fun online gaming with a ton of friends, or even on a server where they can meet new people and have in-depth conversations while enjoying themselves.

They will enjoy a lot of time outdoors. Things like Geo-caching and hiking are classic hobbies for a Sagittarian to get outdoors, spend time with like-minded people, and connect with the elements. Sagittarius natives hate habit, so if it means doing the same thing every Saturday, they'll quickly abandon it and move on to another hobby.

The second thing that Sagittarians need is a good party; regularly, but not scheduled, Sagittarians should go have fun. These events can range from a kickback, bar-b-que, or meet up at a local brewery. They might also include wild nights in the New York party scene, raves in the desert, or barn parties. There's no limit to how often this sun sign can go out, and there are no restrictions on how that fun should happen. They know how to relax, and they know how to have fun.

Parties are a great way for Sagittarians to boost their friends. They help break people out of their shell, and those who would normally stand on the side of the dancefloor looking sheepish are quick to follow a Sagittarian out and do several well-loved dances. Unlike other fire signs, Sagittarians don't consume people with their ego or their intellect; instead, it provokes it in others.

But they need a lot of freedom. If anything feels scheduled or regular, they reject it. They are rebels in the most fundamental way of rebellion. They don't feel the need to do something because someone else said they needed to. However, they don't seek freedom out because of rebellion. It's their nature. Jupiter is the planet of the higher mind. They are in the modality of change and under the element of passionate fire. They passionately love change, so they can grow mentally and develop their understanding of the world.

A Relationship Founded on Trust and Sustained Through Fun

There is a lot of misinformation and mis-attributed belief about Sagittarians when it comes to relationships. Are these characters flighty? Yes. Are they quick to get out of a relationship? Yes. Does it take them a long time to get into a relationship? Usually. Are they more prone to short affairs rather than that one lifelong love? Yes.

But people fail to see the bigger picture. A Sagittarius is loyal, loving, and open. It is often their negative qualities that pull the relationship down, but it is typically the Sagittarius that leaves the relationship, and here is why.

A Sagittarius cannot be anything but themselves, they cannot mask their personality, and they won't try. They are unashamedly who they are, and the world can take it or leave it. So, when they're in a relationship, they're giving what they must give. They offer that loyalty, openness, and love. When they see that their need for freedom, high-energy, and strongly held opinions affect the relationship, they may begin to think it's time to move on. This challenge creates a domino effect where the other person will clutch to the relationship even tighter and become more insecure about their stance. The Sagittarius will often leave because of their needs, and because they know that they aren't helping other person thrive either.

Ultimately, a Sagittarius will find their best match in either a Leo, Aries, or Aquarius. Leo and Aries are obvious choices as they allow for a relationship to grow on the foundation of trust and fun. These other fire signs realize what it means to need space, and they tend to not worry too much about their romantic partner wandering or doing their own thing. Additionally, these signs can both be high energy, and when they're not, they won't mind when the Sagittarius goes off to do something fun without them.

Aquarius is unique. Clearly, it's not a fire sign, but it does have many things in common with a Sagittarius that makes for a great romantic relationship. Foremost, they're both highly independent, and neither will be likely to tell the other what they want to do. Second, Aquarius is also deeply entrenched in the need to explore philosophy and the concepts that drive human belief. These two will have a lot of fun together and not make unreasonable demands of the other person.

Typically, in a relationship, you can expect the Sagittarian to be high energy and to question everything. They crave to know why you love your hobbies or what led you into your career. They're also not impressed with boring answers such as, "well, it's good money" because they need the full story. Additionally, they will want to wander. They may not be unfaithful because Sagittarians are loyal, but they will crave to meet new people and have lively conversations. Sagittarius natives don't have time to put up with jealousy and don't want someone tracking their every move.

Getting down to the biggest issue that people bring up with Sagittarians and relationships: settling down. When do they do it? Usually, when they find the one who lets them be themselves. That sounds cliché, but it's true Sagittarians don't settle down until they've found "the one" who doesn't ask them to negotiate and won't compromise their values or needs either.

The spouse or significant other should expect constant change and fun plans almost non-stop. They should also expect to be open with how trusting they are, and that trust is the relationship's foundation.

Sagittarians thrive when they have a solid partner by their side and when they support each other.

A Career Path That Works on Multiple Levels

Sagittarians need to find satisfaction through their employment, or they'll jump around often. A Sagittarius native will rely on the duality of their zodiac sign to easily move in and out of different environments, and they thrive in the challenge of learning a new position.

Now, a Sagittarius native might need a little push in the right direction from people they respect and trust. Most Sagittarians will find nothing satisfying in entry-level positions, but they experience particular troubles in obtaining all the information necessary and putting in the time to move upward in any specific industry. The struggle they face is that they want to learn everything they can, and they usually do so before they can advance into the next reasonable position.

They need a career where they can be around people who matter and help others improve themselves. Ideally, they will work where each day will bring something new. Even when there is structure, they thrive in high-energy and unpredictable industries that offer a lot of opportunities for problem-solving.

Additionally, a Sagittarius will probably face unique issues with their coworkers. They say what is on their mind, and that can prevent them from moving forward in their career. It may even be an issue of energy where the Sagittarian high intensity is just too much for another coworker, and it can cause conflict.

Countless career paths can put a Sagittarius on the right path with all the right opportunities. But even then, it's likely that the Sagittarius will change careers more often than other signs would during their lifetime.

Make a Plan to Continue Learning

A Sagittarius can't thrive or be happy if they aren't learning in one way or another. One Sagittarius spoken to during the creation of this book pointed out they didn't need to learn anything tangible, only accept new information. So, he avidly listens to audiobooks and podcasts since the radio holds little appeal for him. Another pointed out that they would use the *Great Courses Plus* and take classes on anything that caught their interest.

As the philosopher and the adventurer within the zodiac, there are many times when they don't need a formal plan for book-provided or information-driven education. They will learn through experience, so they choose field trips and cultural programs or opportunities. A Sagittarius would see traveling as the greatest lesson and may make frequent trips to local museums or art centers.

Reel in Those Emotions

Sagittarians are fast to anger as a fire sign, but their modality for change and their Ninth house of the higher mind draw their focus away from that desire to snap. Then, there's the Sagittarian's sudden jump into melancholy if they aren't doing things that align with their core self. If they are stuck in a dead-end job, can't party, don't have fun, and feel caged in by their family or relationship, then they are outright unhappy in every form of the word.

The concern isn't that Sagittarius natives have the opportunity for such big emotions. It's that they have trouble changing speed. They get stuck in one gear, and although they want to change, it can feel as though they're fixed in a rut. This rut could be a lesson given from the planet Jupiter about making your own luck or forcing your own way into a better situation. Remember that both representatives of Jupiter, being Jupiter (Roman God) and Zeus (Greek God), both had to fight to take down their father and become the God of Gods.

These big emotions can feel alarmingly unstable and even make the Sagittarius feel as though their emotions imprison them. When they get mad, they get petty. They will unfriend people on social media and outright ignore those who slighted them. Then, when they are sad, they become emotionally tired and try to flee anything. They may quit their job, refuse to eat, hide in their bedroom for days, or bolt and leave without a word to anyone.

To keep these big emotions from controlling you, you should have a regimen of actions that feed your inner Archer. At least one fun thing, at least one way to connect with new people, and one way to express your humor allowing you to joke with others.

Keep Your Emotions in Check with These Tips

• Do little things that make you happy

• Understand your moon sign – It has a deeper connection with your inner emotions than your sun sign.

• Distance yourself from bystanders when you're at your worst. You lash out, so take the innocent ones out of the picture. Turn to reliable friends, or just get time alone to recharge.

Feel Your Sagittarian Strengths

The best way to ensure that you're living your best life is to move forward with a clear vision and a focus on taking on both physical and intellectual challenges. It's far too common that Sagittarius natives fall to their weakness of poor planning, and because of that, they often don't meet the big goals they have for themselves. Sagittarians thrive when they face big challenges and can push themselves to be even better. They want to see their hard work turn into something useful, and that is the reward. They don't put so much weight into gathering material possessions, so don't overly focus on what you have, but instead, on what you accomplish.

Those born in the Ninth House have a strong ego and are stubborn. If you're the friend, family member, or romantic partner of a Sagittarius, they can be challenging to understand. Their fiercely loyal nature makes it seem as though you should give them more attention, but they want independence and freedom. Their inclination to help others improve themselves makes it appear that they don't need that same support. That is what you can give a Sagittarius to help them thrive. Communicate how clearly you understand that they can accomplish their goals and take on big demands.

With a mindset towards forwarding momentum and an emphasis on big demands and rewards of the higher mind, a Sagittarian can lead one of the best lives possible. They are not so easily affected by their environment and can truly thrive anywhere as they welcome change and new challenges. Sagittarius is among the noblest signs, and it will affect those in their life, often in a positive way. All they crave in return is the freedom to be themselves with a bit of humor in their life.

Conclusion

We hope this book has helped you discover yourself or the Sagittarius native in your life. Sagittarians are complex individuals that put themselves out there for all the world to see. It appears they would be a "what you see is what you get" group but they unknowingly face many challenges in their life they don't understand. Typically, a Sagittarius will flit through life with one passion, one career, one lover after another.

Throughout this guide, we've discovered that the demands they face are often the difficulties of the other person involved in their life. The Sagittarius themselves don't care for what anyone else might think, and often take pride in doing things their own way. With an unmatched desire for freedom and independence, not surprisingly, a few of the world's most notorious political and public figures are Sagittarians. They exude confidence, have magnetic personalities, and, as you've seen here, always approach life with the best-case scenario in mind.

Thank you for reading our guide, and we hope that you have found this helpful in your day-to-day life.

Here's another book by Mari Silva that you might like

THE ULTIMATE GUIDE TO AN AMAZING ZODIAC SIGN IN ASTROLOGY

SCORPIO

MARI SILVA

References

21 Secrets Of The Sagittarius Personality... (2017, October 19). Zodiac Fire. https://zodiacfire.com/sagittarius-personality/

Almanac, O. F. (n.d.). *Mercury Retrograde and Zodiac Signs.* Old Farmer's Almanac. Retrieved from https://www.almanac.com/content/mercury-retrograde-and-zodiac-signs

Angharad. (n.d.). *Male And Female Traits - Sagittarius.* Angharad Reese Celtic Astrology Online. Retrieved from https://www.areeseceltiastrology.com/sagittarius-girl-and-guy-personalities/

Astrology: Mercury in the Signs. (n.d.). Cafeastrology.com. Retrieved from https://cafeastrology.com/articles/mercuryinsigns_page2.html

Astrology.Care - Sagittarius Strengths and Weaknesses, Love, Family, Career, Money. (n.d.). Astrology.Care. Retrieved from http://astrology.care/sagittarius.html

Famous Sagittarius Writers. (n.d.). Www.Thefamouspeople.com. Retrieved November 7, 2020, from https://www.thefamouspeople.com/sagittarius-writers.php

Get to Know Sagittarius. (2014, November 24). Heather Beardsley Coaching. https://hbeardsley.com/get-to-know-sagittarius

Horoscopes. (2017). Bustle. https://www.bustle.com/horoscopes

Kaus Australis (Epsilon Sagittarii): Star System, Name, Constellation | Star Facts. (2019, September 18). Star-Facts.com. https://www.star-facts.com/kaus-australis/

Kaus Borealis. (n.d.). Www.Constellationsofwords.com. Retrieved from https://www.constellationsofwords.com/stars/KausBorealis.html

Keeping A Sagittarius Happy - Astroyogi.com. (n.d.). Www.Astroyogi.com. Retrieved from https://www.astroyogi.com/articles/keeping-a-sagittarius-happy.aspx

Moon in Sagittarius: Characteristics & Personality Traits. (n.d.). Stars Like You. Retrieved from https://www.starslikeyou.com.au/your-astrology-profile/moon-in-sagittarius/

My Sagittarius Zodiac Sign: Love. (n.d.). Www.Horoscope.com. https://www.horoscope.com/zodiac-signs/sagittarius/love

ophiuchus zodiac sign, Ophiuchus Traits, Celebrities, astrology, horoscopes, mythology. (n.d.). Www.Findyourfate.com. Retrieved from https://www.findyourfate.com/astrology/ophiuchus-13zodiac.html

Sagittarius Friendship Compatibility. (n.d.). Tarot.com. Retrieved from https://www.tarot.com/astrology/compatibility/friends/sagittarius

Sagittarius Horoscope: Sagittarius Zodiac Sign Dates Compatibility, Traits and Characteristics. (n.d.). Www.Astrology-Zodiac-Signs.com. https://www.astrology-zodiac-signs.com/zodiac-signs/sagittarius/

Saturn in Sagittarius. (n.d.). Tarot.com. Retrieved from https://www.tarot.com/astrology/planets/saturn-in-sagittarius

Sun in the Signs – Interpretations. (n.d.). Astrolibrary.org. Retrieved from https://astrolibrary.org/interpretations/sun/#sagittarius

The Editors of Encyclopedia Britannica. (2018). Jupiter | Roman god. In *Encyclopædia Britannica.* https://www.britannica.com/topic/Jupiter-Roman-god

The Zodiac Sign Sagittarius. (n.d.). Www.Alwaysastrology.com. Retrieved from https://www.alwaysastrology.com/sagittarius.html

This Is How Your Zodiac Sign Acts At A Party. (n.d.). My.Astrofame.com. Retrieved from https://my.astrofame.com/astrology/article/zodiac-signs-party

Top 10 Sagittarius Jobs | Money & Career | Ask Astrology Blog. (2018, November 21). Ask Astrology. https://askastrology.com/top-10-sagittarius-jobs/